THE COOPERSTOWN REVIEW

THE FORUM OF BASEBALL LITERARY OPINION

VOLUME TWO

Edited by Paul Adomites

Sheraden Publishing, Pittsburgh, Pennsylvania

ISBN # 1-882974-03-4
Sheraden Publishing, Pittsburgh, Pa 15204

Editorial consultants: Luke Salisbury and Dick Johnson.
Designed by Pati Ingold.
Cover Illustration by Bob Carroll.
Borders by Moreau, Inc.
Printed by Mathews Printing Corporation, Pittsburgh, Pa.
Thanks to the Society for American Baseball Research.

In this issue...

"You begin to see the Game as at once a precise mirror of where we are in this country and at the same time this one thing that seems a constant not of this time."
Ken Burns "Interview," page 94

"'Shoeless Joe' blazed an economic trail for baseball fiction... Schmalz it and they will come."
Luke Salisbury, Baseball Fiction Hall of Fame, page 45

"Baseball is simply a matter of rooting faithfully (and in most cases and for most seasons, quite hopelessly) for the cherished hometown nine."
Peter C. Bjarkman, "Team Histories," page 161

"If you're a Believer it isn't necessary to explain, and if you're not, volumes won't do the trick."
Ed Goldstein on Mickey Mantle books, page 79

"I had to create something worthy of Aaron, worthy of Zwilling, worthy of everyone whose dream it was to be on that list, a list every bit as important as the one held by the keeper of the Pearly Gates."
Paul White on The Macmillan Baseball Encyclopedia, page 16

"Toward one end of the huge space of the warehouse, amidst the clickety-clack of the keyboards and the endless scroll of paper being spat out of the printers, a row of dusty wooden file cabinets stand, overflowing with sundry boxscores, newspaper clippings, graphs and charts. On the wall behind the cabinets, right behind the row of ash-trays growing gray tentacled colonies of cigarette butts, there will be a picture of Bill James."
John Roca on Bill James' "The Politics of Glory," page 84

From the Editor

1994 seems to be the year of reference works in the field of baseball publishing. Reference books you'll find reviewed here are Jim Riley's compendious "Biographical Encyclopedia of the Negro Leagues," Lloyd Johnson and Miles Woolf's The Minor League Encyclopedia, David Nemec's encyclopedic-in-import, if not in style "The Rules of Baseball," and Dewey and Acocella's "Encyclopedia of Major League Team Histories." Another big-book effort comes from the always entertaining Paul Dickson in his "The Worth Book of Softball." Two reference books not reviewed in this issue are Westcott and Bilovsky's immense and enjoyable The New Phillies Encyclopedia, and the culmination of SABR's longtime research into Blackball, "The Negro Leagues." In addition, that mammoth company named Microsoft is releasing "Complete Baseball," a CD- ROM adventure. High-tech baseball lovers are drooling.

In this issue we begin the process of selecting "The Baseball Fiction Hall of Fame." The first thing we did was poll the experts; now we want to hear from you. See page 45.

OTHER NEWS: Frequent contributor to THE REVIEW, Jim Sumner has written "Separating the Men from the Boys: The First Half-Century of the Carolina League"(John F. Blair). Bruce Chadwick and David Spindel are continuing their fine team memorabilia series with new books on the Cubs and the Reds. And Marc Okkonen has done it again with his volume on the Game in the 1950s: wonderful work, Marc; keep it up.

Because they aren't hamstrung by the big market demands, college and university presses are publishing some of the more interesting volumes on baseball. This year Texas A&M University Press has released "The Meaning of Nolan Ryan" (reviewed on page 127) and Richard Skolnick's "Baseball and the Pursuit of Innocence." Wayne

State University has published Richard Bak's "Turkey Stearnes and the Detroit Stars." At the University of Nebraska Press, they're continuing their terrific series of reprints, this year bringing back three we've missed: Harry "Steamboat" Johnson's "Standing the Gaff: The Life and Times of a Minor League Umpire," Larry Gerlach's groundbreaking "The Men in Blue," and Ted Vincent's "The Rise and Fall of American Sport: Mudville's Revenge." Dan Ross tells us that next year they will be publishing two new volumes, both what he calls "documentary histories." One is "Sol White's History of Coloured Baseball"; the other is "A Documentary History of Baseball, 1825-1908" by Dean Sullivan. There's great news from Penn State University Press: David Voigt, first-stringer among the Game's great historians is finishing a book on the American Association, and after that he will continue his multi-volume history of the sport. All lovers of baseball history are looking forward to Voigt's new work.

Big biographies of big baseball legends have become hot items. Joining recent volumes on Ruth and Williams is Richard Bak's "Ty Cobb: His Tumultuous Life and Times" (Taylor). Walker and Company has issued the Glenn Stout/Dick Johnson masterpiece on The Splinter in paperback for just $12.95, and have announced that the same two gents will create a similar book on Joe DiMaggio.

Others we missed are Gai Ingham Berlage's "Women in Baseball: The Forgotten History" (Praeger) and Terry Pluto's "The Curse of Rocky Colavito: A Loving Look at a Thirty-Year Slump" (Simon & Schuster). If baseball's restructuring means the end of the great pennant races, Dave Anderson has covered them all for you in "Pennant Races: Baseball At Its Best" (Doubleday).

Thanks especially to Tom Conrad of Conrad & Company, and as always, to the woman who makes all the difference in the world -- Rosemary.

-- Paul Adomites

CONTENTS

ESSAYS

If You Love Baseball, You'll Love SABR

Since 1971, Society for American Baseball Research members have been providing their fellow members and fans around the world with fascinating insights into baseball's history, lore, statistics and literature. In 1993, SABR members will receive:

- the **Baseball Research Journal**, a 96 page annual filled with statistical analysis & essays,
- **The National Pastime**, an 88 page annual featuring entertaining articles and photographs,
- a new publication from SABR's Baseball Records Committee and a reissue of historic literature from baseball's past,
- a Membership Directory listing over 6,000 members,
- a monthly newsletter, *The SABR Bulletin,*
- member discounts.

PLUS, regional and national meetings, and 14 research committees, from ballparks to women in baseball. Whether you become an active researcher, or just enjoy the wonderful publications and membership benefits, SABR membership is perfect for the knowledgeable baseball fan.

SABR • P.O. Box 93183 • Dept. ML2 • Cleveland, OH 44101
(216) 575-0500

YES! I want to join SABR! I am enclosing a check or money order ($35 U.S., $45 Canada & Mexico, $50 overseas, U.S. funds or foreign equivalent) to SABR for a 1993 membership.

Name ___________________________

Address ___________________________

City _____________________ State ______ ZIP __________

Phone ___________________________

Baseball on the Mean Streets

By Howard Elson

THE "NEAR NORTH" neighborhood of Chicago was first settled by the English even before Chicago became a city in 1837. It was home to successive waves of poorer and poorer immigrants, Irish, Swedes, Sicilians, and Southern Blacks, until 1942 when, in an attempt to revitalize the area, by then beset with poverty, filth, crime and violence, the city of Chicago bulldozed the decrepit wood-frame shanties and built the first rowhouses of what would eventually become the second largest housing project in the United States, Cabrini-Green.

Tenant applicants to the project were screened carefully to ensure family stability. Unseemly behavior like littering and walking on the grass were punishable by fines. Supermarkets, department stores, restaurants and banks soon took

HARDBALL:
A Season in the Projects
by Daniel Coyle
Putnam, 1994, $29.95

hold. Children rollerskated at the high school and shot baskets in the playgrounds. In the '50s and early '60s the projects expanded, with 15, then eight high rise apartments. They were clean and everything in them worked, even the elevators.

The Cabrini-Green projects were a model of successful public housing and urban planning.

In 1969 the Federal government fixed public housing tenant rates at 25% of income. This effectively drove out the most stable people living in the projects, working class families who could find cheaper rents in private apartments. The poorest, least desirable segment of the tenant population stayed. They had to.

At the same time, the American Civil Liberties Union brought suits severely restricting the applicant screening process and making it extremely difficult to evict troublesome tenants. The Chicago Housing Authority director was accused of widespread financial impropriety and a Department of Housing and Urban Development study concluded that only five of nineteen project managers were competent and knowledgeable, and that the Housing Authority was operating in a state of profound confusion and disarray.

Still, in April 1969, when Martin Luther King, Jr. was assassinated, riots engulfed all the projects and black neighborhoods in Chicago except for Cabrini-Green, where residents grieved in relative peace. Thousands of people were burned out and displaced. It was decided to forego any screening and simply move whole blocks of burned out and homeless residents into vacant apartments in Cabrini-Green, despite protests that many of these families had gang connections, connections heretofore foreign to the Cabrini-Green projects. The Cobra Stones, a branch of the notorious Blackstone Rangers, the Vice Lords, the Blacks, the Deuces Wild, and the Gangster Disciples all took up residence in Cabrini-Green. From then on, the projects became a war zone of drugs, killings, sniper attacks, ambushes, nightly shooting, assaults, rape, terror, intimidation, and murder.

Today, Cabrini-Green sits eleven blocks from the famous Loop of downtown Chicago, and four blocks from the fabled "Gold Coast," second only to Manhattan's upper East Side as the nation's wealthiest city neighborhood. Cabrini-Green sits like a festering abscess, our own Sarajevo on the shores of the Chicago River, the Beirut of America's heartland.

An unlikely setting, to be sure, for a book chronicling the trials and tribulations, defeats and victories in the season of one Little League team, but that is what Daniel Coyle, senior editor for Outside magazine, has written.

It is the true story of the Near North Kikuyus, named, as are all the teams in this, the only sanctioned Little League based in a housing project, for an indigenous African people. Sponsored by one of Chicago's largest financial institutions, the Kikuyus are a team of poor black 9-12 year old boys coached by a group of "white, college educated young men with short hair, suburban backgrounds, and orthodontically corrected teeth."

To his credit, Daniel Coyle does not give us what might be expected, the "there but for the grace of baseball go I," heartwarming saga of a group of black children triumphing over their deprived circumstances while their white mentors gain a new understanding and compassion for those less fortunate than they.

He does however chronicle, very honestly, without rendering judgment, without drawing conclusions, what it's like being a kid, in an almost impossible to survive, impossible to escape situation. The Bad News Bears it's not.

If this book were a novel, it would be a bad one. If it were a movie it would be even worse. All the characters are all cliches, so predictable in their behavior, stereotypes obviously meant to depict, in one individual, a whole set of group characteristics. That they are in fact, real people in real situations is a big part of what makes this book so fascinating.

We are introduced to Bob Muzikowski, the former coke sniffing, alcoholic "golden boy" of Columbia University who is now a very successful "born-again" insurance salesman, cool, organized and disciplined yet with a seething, dangerous temper hidden just under the devout, calm surface. Bob is the guiding force behind the league. We also meet Al Carter, a community activist who has devoted himself to organizing and helping the disadvantaged, but a man who has seen enough racism, disappointment and unfulfilled good intentions in his life so as to color his outlook on everything. Behind every beneficent gesture he sees ulterior motive, behind every innocent suggestion he sees prejudice and bigotry. Quick to take credit, slow to assume responsibility, he cynically clashes with the volunteer coaches at every turn, and is now being accused of personally benefiting from money allocated to the youth organization bearing his name. Al Carter is who the pundit had in mind when he said, "just because you are paranoid doesn't mean somebody isn't really out to get you."

The most fascinating people that Daniel Coyle writes about are the players themselves. The most fascinating, and yet the most discouraging. Children who have learned, or have been taught to survive by utilizing behavior that is so negative, so demeaning, so destructive. They are defiant, defeatist, egocentric, cruel, and boastful. They belittle everyone around them, and immediately threaten surrender when the smallest incident goes against them. These kids don't need baseball, they need therapy. They are severely dysfunctional in a severely dysfunctional environment. It is incredible that the coaches, who put up with this behavior game after game, practice after poorly attended practice don't throw up their hands and walk away. But they don't, and neither does the reader for somehow he knows that if he doesn't care what happens to these kids, no one will.

Because Daniel Coyle offers no answers, no solutions to the problems he so vividly describes in the

projects, this is not an easy book to read. It is disturbing, and discouraging. The conflicts between the well meaning but somewhat naive volunteer coaches and local activist Carter are extremely uncomfortable to witness. As sympathetic as the reader may be to the awful plight of the Kikuyu players, their behavior evokes nothing so much as anger and frustration.

The description of life in the projects is harrowing. A ten year old boy has to figure out new routes home from the candy store because a rival gang has taken over the building he usually goes past; school schedules and room assignments are manipulated so as to minimize contact between rival gang factions; young children try to figuratively make themselves invisible when walking past children affiliated with rival gangs by slowing down, getting small and putting a blank, emotionless look on their face.

Of course like most baseball books, this one isn't really about baseball either. Rather, it uses baseball as its standing place, its point of view from which to see the landscape, a landscape of frustration, seemingly without solution.

"Hardball: A Season in the Projects" is an important, extremely well written book that should find wide readership among people interested in trying to understand what really goes on in a part of America few of us have first hand knowledge about. It is however, a difficult book to read. It is also a difficult book to stop thinking about, because it describes so many seemingly unsolvable issues. We have thrown money at these problems, we have thrown programs at these problems. Things have only gotten worse.

W hat Coyle and his friends have tried to do is to throw people at these problems, and therein may lie the answer. At the end of the season, when almost in spite of their efforts, they do make the playoffs only to be crushed in the championship game, the coaches held a party for the team. At that party, despite all the frustrations of the season, the coaches and the players paired off for the Community Youth Creative Learning Center tutorial program. Once a week, every Monday night, from seven to eight thirty, one coach works with one player helping him with his schoolwork. It may not sound like much, but you have to give the coaches and players credit, it may work... one kid at a time.

HOWARD ELSON, a pediatric dentist by profession, pitches for the Pittsburgh All-Stars, twice national champions of the Men's Senior Baseball League Over 30.

The Man Behind the Mask

By Bill Carle

FEW MAJOR LEAGUE BASE-ball players lead lives fascinating enough that they merit a full-length biography. We are enthralled by their exploits on the diamond and we revere them as the heroes of our youth, and as such, their lives are objects of curiosity. Reading about their lives brings them off the Mount Olympus of the playing field and allows us to see them as ordinary people. However, the key word in that sentence is "ordinary." The only reason that these players interest us at all is because of their extraordinary feats of baseball brilliance. For the most part, aside from their baseball career, their lives are ordinary, in fact, even mundane. But Morris Berg was one major league player who, in spite of a rather ordinary baseball career, led a life that was as captivating and yet confusing as anyone in recent memory, baseball player or not.

Although Moe Berg was a career .243 hitter over a 15-year playing career ending in 1939, his name was familiar to me even as a child. I had heard stories of Berg being a spy during World War II and his photos from Japan being the key to successful bombing missions of that country. I had heard that Berg spoke seven languages and was one of the most intelligent men ever to play major league baseball. In this meticulously researched study, Nicholas Dawidoff examines every aspect of Berg's life, exposing both fact and myth along the way in one of the most fascinating and interesting biographies I have ever read.

Dawidoff literally must have interviewed virtually every living soul who came into contact with Berg throughout his life. As a result we feel we are accompanying Berg

---

THE CATCHER WAS A SPY
By Nicholas Dawidoff
Pantheon Books, 1994, 348 pp.

along his life's journey, traveling with him to exotic lands, and wondering how this man could charm and yet frustrate all the famous scientists, athletes, writers, and statesmen he encountered along the way.

Berg's life contains a myriad of contradictions. He was a fine ballplayer at Princeton and genuinely loved the game. It was important for him to make the major leagues yet he seldom played and didn't seem to care whether he did. In fact, his major league career is so austere, it is amazing that he stayed in the majors for 15 years.

Berg received a law degree yet he never practiced law. He understood medicine, physics, politics, and several languages, yet never held a full-time job and seldom earned any money. Berg was Jewish and sensitive to anti-Semitism, yet joined mostly Christian organizations and attended far more Christian services than Jewish. Berg knew an incredible array of famous people from all walks of life, such as Albert Einstein, Nelson Rockefeller, Anita Loos, and Chico Marx, yet was always described as a loner. Berg longed for praise and recognition, yet the one major honor he received, the Medal of Freedom, he refused to accept.

Our travels with Berg take us to the Sorbonne in Paris, where he studied upon his graduation from Princeton. We go to a geisha house in Japan with Berg and Babe Ruth. It was on this Japanese trip that Berg dressed up in a kimono, and smuggled a camera to the top of a hospital to take pictures of downtown Tokyo. We accompany Berg throughout Europe as he uses his intellect and charm to learn the secrets of Nazi Germany's struggles to build the atomic bomb. We watch amused as Berg unsuccessfully tries to explain baseball to Albert Einstein. Finally, we literally roam the streets through the pitiable latter years of Berg's life as he sponges off the many acquaintances he has made over the years by using his charm and storytelling to gain food and lodging.

The more I traveled with Berg, the more I wondered how Berg could fashion a life such as this. I found myself trying to look at his upbringing and family as well as his education to see if I could figure it out. In his final chapter, Dawidoff does the same thing and provides a

very plausible theory to explain the mystery behind the mysterious Moe Berg.

Dawidoff obviously did an incredible amount of research on Moe Berg. He interviewed ballplayers, actors, scientists, family members, and secret agents. Dawidoff has a first-rate command of the English language and his writing is solid throughout although it would prove helpful to keep a dictionary handy. Words such as "crepuscular", "quotidian", and "philology" are not words one encounters in a typical baseball book. However, "The Catcher Was a Spy" is not really a baseball book; it is a captivating biography about a fascinating man, who happened to play major league baseball. It is, quite simply, one of the best biographies I have read.

BILL CARLE is chairman of SABR's Biographical Committee, which specializes in tracking down ballplayers for the historical record.

Trying to Match the Magic

By Paul White

Editor's note: 1994 is the 25th anniversary of an event that changed the face of baseball fandom forever, and as inexorably as Babe Ruth changed the game on the field. It was the publication of The Baseball Encyclopedia by Macmillan. That immense tome appeared to be the end-all of baseball statistics. Little did we know it was only the beginning of a glorious new age for fans of the Game. In recognition of this historic event, THE REVIEW asked Paul White, editor of USA Today Baseball Weekly, to recall for our readers what first seeing the Encyclopedia meant for him.

STORED SOMEWHERE IN MY HOME IS A BOX THAT ONCE CONtained cowboy boots. The box has been in spare rooms, under beds and in closets; it has made the treks from New York to Iowa to New York to Michigan to Virginia — and plenty of shorter hauls in between.

I don't even remember how long it's been since I opened that red and brown carton, and whenever it was, I probably just poked my finger through the papers inside, wondering if I would ever again take up what I once believed to be the most important project of my life.

I'm sure I thought I would eventually dive headlong into that box, and maybe I still harbor some hope I will.

You see, that box contains the greatest baseball tournament of all

time, one with all the greats of the game (at least the ones who played before 1969). It's a tournament stuck in time, in first-round limbo for two decades or more.

And it all sprouted from my introduction to the Baseball Encyclopedia. All those pages, all those names, all those numbers. Awestruck by the scope of what lay opened in front of me, I had to create something worthy of Aaron, worthy of Zwilling, worthy of everyone whose dream was to be on that list, a list every bit as important as the one held by the keeper of the Pearly Gates.

No matter that none of them knew the list would exist in the form I saw it that day. The honor it carried was its importance, the honor that "major leaguer" would forever be attached to those names.

So, I created an elimination tournament to be played on one of the board games I had. I chose the game whose rating formula I figured I had pretty much approximated during my pre-fantasy league days, days in which I knew I was hard-core because I abandoned dice and spinners and purchased books of random numbers designated for the games, days when I would throw a tantrum if my cat had the audacity to amble across the papers and cards strewn on the family room floor.

I counted the names in the Encyclopedia. Why? Because I had no idea if I had a player pool that would create 64 team rosters, or 128, or 256. It turned out 128 would work just fine.

So I went to work creating the roster. It was simple at the start. Henry Aaron went to Team 1, Tommie Aaron to Team 2, etc. Hmm, the teams couldn't be identified just by number, so I found a list of the 128 largest U.S. cities. It was New York for Hank, Chicago (the 1960 census was still in force) was Tommie.

This is where the magic of the Encyclopedia took hold. As in earlier years when I was mesmerized by the record book (I could pore through the no-hitter listings for hours, especially the unusual ones the so-called purists have tried to legislate out of existence). I found myself looking at names, nicknames, birthplaces, unexplainably quirky careers.

It took seemingly forever to compile my list, weeks I'm sure.

Of course in such a random assignment of players, some teams came up lacking at positions, so I had to go back and make arbitrary but essentially balanced trades to fill the gaps.

Then it was on to the actual games. Each matchup was a best- of-seven series, and I kept track on handmade scorecards scribbled on the backs of used paper my mother brought home from work.

As I said, I barely got into the middle of the first round when college and marriage and all sorts of other things interfered.

Was I crazy? No, inspired. It was simply the only thing I could dream up big enough to merit the scope of this book.

Will I ever get back to it? If I do, I suspect I'll start over. The tournament was OK, but getting there through the pages of the Encyclopedia was the real fun.

Besides, as soon as I get to Shawn Abner, the whole face of the game will change.

PAUL WHITE is the editor of USA Today Baseball Weekly.

Rhinestones

By John Pastier

WHEN HOLLYWOOD needs an old ballpark, it won't hesitate to cast a minor leaguer in the role. In "A League of Their Own," Bosse Field was painted to resemble the Rockford Peaches' home. War Memorial Stadium became the home of the mythical New York Knights in "The Natural," and Owen Bush Stadium was passed off as Comiskey Park in 1919 for "Eight Men Out."

When major publishers take on ballparks, a similar plan emerges. They have faith that packaging and marketing can turn Double-A material into a major league product. In 1992, this tactic was used for "Lost Ballparks" and "Green Cathedrals," astutely reviewed here last year by book editor Glenn Stout. He found "a cynical `this is good enough, because after all, people

> **DIAMONDS:**
> **The Evolution of the Ballpark**
> **From Elysian Fields**
> **to Camden Yards**
> By Michael Gershman
> Houghton Mifflin, 1993, 259 pp.,
> $39.95

love ballparks' attitude" represented in these books, and objected to "publishers who...disrespect their audience" by palming off glitzy packages as solid accomplishments.

At the end of the 1993 baseball season, Michael Gershman's more ambitious "Diamonds" appeared. It aimed to be the first chronological and structured stadium history, not just a series of listings or essays arranged by city. This was clear from its subtitle, "The Evolution of the Ballpark," and from dust jacket avowals that its "unique approach focuses on the historical development of these special places...the most complete and accurate history ever compiled on ballparks...a rich blend of meticulously researched history, illuminating anecdotes, and ...rare photographs, evocative maps, diagrams, and illustrations... 'Diamonds' tells

this story with eloquence and authority...the result of four years of research, travel, and an encyclopedic knowledge of baseball memorabilia."

Gershman was once a rock and roll publicist. He is now a baseball-project entrepreneur with good publishing connections, and has assembled several engagement calendars and two ballpark postcard reproduction booklets. He is an affable fellow with a knack for expressing himself easily in person and in print. Are these qualifications adequate? At first glance, probably not. After studying the book, the answer can only be no.

The key to this book's failings is the word "compilation" in its jacket blurb. Lists and directories are compiled, but histories are researched from reliable sources and carefully synthesized and documented by trained professionals. My dictionary gives the origins of the word "compile" as "to heap together, plunder, plagiarize, pile up." Plagiarize is too strong a word, but the others surely apply. "Diamonds" fails to identify and analyze stadium relationships and influences; it is an accumulation of anecdotal material, heaped together by time period, and piled up without undue regard for relevance. Not enough of it is new or original, and much of what it borrows from others isn't properly

identified as to source.

Like many predecessors, "Diamonds" is unreliable, but its degree of unreliability is especially severe. Nearly every page of text has at least one unsupported, questionable, or flatly wrong statement, and its value judgments often lack credibility. "Diamonds" claims that South Side Park "is, in fact, a near replica of the grandstand at West Side Grounds," when one Chicago park is shown as a single-deck stand and the other as a double-decked one. Unsubstantiated assertions that a given park was "undistinguished," "was even less notable," "was no great shakes," "wasn't much of a park," "was unremarkable," "unremarkable despite its longevity," or "unremarkable in any way," say more about weak powers of observation and analysis than about the parks themselves. At times Gershman ignores his own manuscript. Observing Cincinnati's Palace of the Fans, he sighs that "the ballpark, formerly a democratic venue [now] had opera boxes for beer-swilling patrons," yet approvingly notes that Chicago's earlier Lakefront Park "set new standards for fan comfort with its private boxes." Why was elitism laudable in 1883 but not in 1902? Although "The first grandstands built solely for paying sports customers" emerged soon after 1821, the same page states that in the 1830s "All sports events were, literally, stand-

ing room only." We hear that "Camden Yards is the most innovative and influential major league ballpark since Yankee Stadium," but his discussion of the Bronx stadium mentions no influence that it may have had on other parks. Factual errors abound. Some originate with the author, while others are taken uncritically from earlier publications. He writes that Abraham Lincoln's funeral train stopped at the B&O warehouse at Camden Yards, but the warehouse was built about four decades later. He says that hitters at The Yards "will have to launch a ball 460 feet to right center to earn a home run and 432 feet down the line..." (The true figures are more than 100 feet shorter.) Candlestick Park is called "the first [ballpark] made entirely of reinforced concrete" (even the doors, seats, windows and handrails?), when that structural distinction belongs to Baltimore's Memorial Stadium, built six years earlier.

"Diamonds" flunks geography: Los Angeles' Washington Park was not at 8th and Hill Streets, in the heart of downtown, but was more than a mile away, well outside the business district, and there was never a ballpark at Eighth and Hill. Gershman puts the first paid admission game in Newtown, and adds that "Newtown is now Flushing Meadows, Queens, which means the park was less than three hundred yards from Shea Stadium." Newtown is not in Flushing Meadows, and is two miles southwest of Shea. Nor did 23rd Street run behind Shibe Park's right field wall — that was 20th.

> **Gershman roundly dislikes domes, multi-purpose venues, circular stadiums and artificial turf (don't we all?), but his stance seems based more on prejudice than familiarity.**

The book's scope is damagingly narrow. It excludes minor league and college parks, and effectively ignores many active and even important major league venues. Royals Stadium was the first permanent park to reject the large-capacity, multi-purpose paradigm of the 1960s and '70s, and is notable as the model for Pilot Field, New Comiskey, the first Camden Yards design (which is also omitted), and other unbuilt proposals. It also gave birth to today's Big Three stadium architects. But it is not discussed at all in the text, nor are several indoor venues.

Gershman roundly dislikes domes, multi-purpose venues, circular stadiums and artificial turf (don't we all?), but his stance seems based more on prejudice than familiarity. Last year, he told a reporter that he's never seen a game on a rug, other than watching a contest at Veterans Stadium for 20 minutes before walking out in disgust. Thus, "Diamonds'" meticulous researcher has no useful first-hand experience with at least ten of the 28 current ML parks. (And probably more, based on a chat in which Gershman resisted my suggestion that round parks are not identical, and that visiting them would be enlightening.) He calls the Astrodome and Metrodome "sunless" even though their translucent roofs admit considerable daylight. He grumbles that the Astrodome "cut baseball off from its natural medium —oxygen," but doesn't supply any data on fan, player, or peanut vendor asphyxiation.

Olympic Stadium is the largest, most expensive, tallest and most structurally complex baseball park, the first with a retractable roof, the only active one to see Olympic use, and the only one with an integral subway station. We learn none of

this in "Diamonds," which allots it no text, one photo, and a caption comparing it to "an industrial-strength clamshell." Gershman has not seen it, nor the "baseball on the half-shell" SkyDome (the only other foreign ML park, an attendance-record holder, the second-most costly park, and the first with a reliably movable roof and true mixed-use occupancy), since neither has natural grass.

He calls Veterans Stadium round, despite its very different and more complex shape of eight arcs, like Jack Murphy Stadium. Termed a superellipse or an octorad, it's a compromise between a square and a circle, and yields a better configuration than either for baseball and football. This geometric astigmatism covers 19 centuries, since he also ascribes roundness to the elliptical Roman Colosseum.

Jack Murphy Stadium appears only in two lists of dates and dimensions. There is not one illustration or word of text in this "most complete and accurate history ever compiled on ballparks" devoted to the best example of architecture among big-league parks of the last 70 years. This powerfully sculpted and structurally integrated work is the only stadium ever to win a national building design award from the American Institute of Architects. To top things off, its original

center-field distance is understated by 15 feet in one list (but not the other), perhaps because the true figure of 420 feet would weaken that list's contention that 15 modern "parks are nearly identical."

"Diamonds" never comes to grips with stadium design as an art or as a science. There is no discussion of architectural space, detailing, geometric typologies, or structural expression. There is no coherent attempt to trace design influences, although the author maintains, with a straight face, that the Huntington Avenue Grounds "influenced ballpark architecture" (i.e., Camden Yards) because "clearly [Baltimore's] architects were aware of the Boston Storage Warehouse behind the left- and left-center field stands." This is like saying that the Polo Grounds influenced the SkyDome by being near water. Gershman implies that Frank Lloyd Wright invented reinforced concrete, and that his Unity Temple inspired team owners to build their stadiums in that material. Neither allusion is accurate.

Architectural perspectives are called models, and structural terms are repeatedly misused or comically mangled (what the author calls "curved columns" are known to the rest of the world as arches). Important structural principles are flatly misstated. Gershman insists that cantilevering (the practice, used in every non-wooden park of the last

hundred years, of projecting the upper decks and roofs beyond the columns and toward the field) puts fans farther from the game. On the contrary, it puts them closer. He also claims that grandstands of the last two decades were steep because they were "built without supporting posts," when they were held up by

Another photo purports to show "the architectural detailing on the third deck" of the double-decked Polo Grounds.

columns, just as in earlier parks. Stadium architects are rarely identified, and their body of work goes unexplored. The Osborn Engineering Company, designer of eleven classic parks and three postwar ones, is barely mentioned, and then only in the context of its Cleveland and Yankee Stadium work. HOK Sport, architects of Pilot Field, Joe Robbie Stadium, New Comiskey, Camden Yards, and the new parks in Cleveland and Denver, doesn't appear in the index, nor do the

names of any others (besides Osborn) of the more than 30 known major-league stadium architects. (HOK is mentioned as having "built Three Rivers Stadium and Veterans Stadium," neither of which is true.) In a book that purports to be a history of an entire building type, overlooking the creators of those buildings is a massive and inexcusable omission. Although Osborn's work forms the core of the classic era that Gershman prefers over all others, he did not visit its archives, nor interview any of its staff. Indeed, there is no sign that he interviewed any stadium architects at all.

This last is only one of many problems with the research and documentation methods of "Diamonds." Scholarly apparatus is woefully lacking for a book claiming to be a history. Its bibliography lists no articles in architectural or engineering publications, nor the basic manifesto on ballpark and urban design philosophy, Philip Bess' "City Baseball Magic." No author appears in the bibliography more than twice, with one exception: Michael Gershman earns eight listings. What he does repeatedly is quote or borrow from secondary and tertiary sources, particularly sportswriters. Obvious primary sources such as stadium designers, architectural and structural blueprints, and even the tangible evidence of many of the stadiums themselves, are ignored completely.

"Diamonds'" documentation is meager. There are no footnotes or endnotes, so it's usually impossible to tell where information or misinformation originates. Some quoted statements aren't attributed to anyone, and there is borrowed research that is uncredited. The index covers only names, and even then is inaccurate and very incomplete.

The writing style in "Diamonds" is not concise. At times it seems that the author is trying to fill up space, or gloss over some dubious informational underpinnings. Its chatty tone, doubtless meant to be ingratiating, can be annoying: we are constantly being asked to "consider" or "note" things, and the overuse of italics to give emphasis seems patronizing. Consistency and balance are also lacking; while many parks are omitted, others are treated at excessive length, perhaps reflecting the easy availability of recyclable material.

Of course, any book of 250 large pages will have its moments. For me, the finest was the opening of Gershman's tribute to "the best park left": "Some parks are hitters' parks. Some parks are pitchers' parks. Fenway is a writer's park." Like Bucky Dent's gossamer homer, that remark cleared the left-field wall. If only there were more such felicitous touches. Some of the

book's 19th century material, both illustrations and contemporary accounts of the parks, yields valuable information. Indeed, the 19th century seems better done than the 20th, but this view may be due to my limited knowledge of the earlier period.

Illustrations are a mixed bag. Many are very good, and some are new to my eyes. Unhappily, though many come from colored postcards, none are reproduced in color, and most do not read well in black and white. Some are poorly chosen, such as the nearly identical pair on page 107 that are obviously retouchings of the same photo. Park diagrams are scarce; there should have been about ten times as many. There are some fine period engravings and Marc Okkonen's invaluable maps and perspective drawings of old parks in context, but no graphics were commissioned for this book. In terms of illustrations, "Diamonds" takes but does not give back.

Book designer Jennie Bush weakens the illustrations' effectiveness by pursuing a nostalgic look. Gratuitous borders, sometimes sporting line drawings of baseballs, gloves, caps, or hot dogs on their corners, trivialize the material and often reduce its size. Many illustrations are annoyingly overlapped by others, by captions, or by diamond-shaped graphic devices that open each chapter. Quite a few

are fuzzy or murky, often due to unwise enlargement. The size of photos and drawings seems unrelated to sharpness or importance, and reproduction is not as crisp as one would expect from a $40 book.

Captioning doesn't help matters. Here the writing flirts with inanity, overlooking meaningful details or significant content in the pictures while zeroing in on trivia such as advertising signs, or irrelevancies such as a water tank near the Polo Grounds that we are asked to "note" on two different occasions for no given reason. Gershman claims that a photo of Baker Bowl "gives a good view of the tracks of the Philadelphia & Reading Railroad", but those tracks actually ran in a tunnel under the field. Another photo purports to show "the architectural detailing on the third deck" of the double-decked Polo Grounds.

"Diamonds'" flaws extend beyond authorial inadequacy. Permissive editing, inattentive indexing and proofreading, and willful design also take their toll. Assessing Orioles Park, Gershman warns that "all the clever repackaging won't turn Camden Yards into Ebbets, Fenway, or Wrigley." He is sensitive to minor applied nostalgia in what he admits is the best ballpark in two generations, yet doesn't recognize that "Diamonds" is held together by a veneer of packaging and marketing capability that won't turn it into a true history.

It's time to invoke Glenn Stout once again, since his 1993 review identified the problems of major-publisher ballpark books so accurately, and uncannily anticipated Gershman's volume. Now there are three books about which one can say: "Under this veneer of history, none treats its subject with real respect. There is a cynical...attitude in each, an attitude that does not contribute to the historical legacy each depends on for its success and purports to honor... Each ersatz volume showed promise to be something else, but is not..."

"Diamonds" is the worst culprit, since it claims greater substance than the others, yet all it really does is lead its readers more thoroughly astray. It is more disturbing than the others because it commands greater resources: it has more and larger pages, more pictures, and costs more than Ritter's or Lowry's works, while dispensing more errors and misinformation than those two combined. (The above recitation of inaccuracies is only an introduction to the subject.)

But that's just one opinion. "Diamonds" is selling very well, thank you, and was recently named the best baseball book of 1993 by a panel of judges having no ballpark expertise. Most people who see this book will be impressed by it, and that can only fortify the publishing industry's faith, shared by some stadium architects, that nostalgia and slick packaging count more than substance.

JOHN PASTIER is an architecture critic who has written about baseball stadiums since 1973, and a ballpark consultant whose work includes Camden Yards and the new Mercer County Stadium in Trenton, N.J. He was awarded a fellowship for ballpark design research by the National Endowment for the Arts, and has studied more than 200 parks in the U.S. and Canada.

The Visual Record

By Luke Salisbury

PHOTOGRAPHS ARE KEY TO baseball memory and "Baseball's Golden Age: The Photographs of Charles M. Conlon" is a fine addition to the record. A comprehensive history of baseball's visual representation has yet to be written, but when it is, Charles Conlon's work will be prominent. Conlon was a proofreader for the New York Telegram who took baseball photographs for extra cash and the chance to get out of the office. He took his first baseball photo in 1904 of Christy Mathewson at the Polo Grounds, and continued taking baseball photographs until 1942. As Neal McCabe's introduction says, "He photographed everyone at the ballpark: players, managers, coaches. umpires, owners, visiting celebrities, wives and children." Many of the glass photographic plates,

---

**BASEBALL'S GOLDEN AGE:
THE PHOTOGRAPHS OF
CHARLES M. CONLON**
By Neal McCabe
and Constance McCabe
Harry N. Abrams, 1993, 198 pp.

---

which preceded film, were lost, broken or thrown away by Conlon, but thousands remain and Neal McCabe and his sister, Constance McCabe, a photograph conservator who works at the National Gallery of Art, have presented a wonderful selection, beautifully reproduced, nicely arranged, and the black and white images are so sharp, they seem to breathe.

My quibbles are with the non-visual elements. Neal McCabe wrote an introduction and each photograph has a caption ranging from a hundred to 250 words. The title is troubling. The time covered is 1904 till 1942. Other than the absence of blacks, what does baseball in 1942 have in common with baseball in 1904? Not enough to qualify it as one age, let alone anoint the whole span a "Golden Age," unless one thinks that the

absence of blacks made it "golden," which I most assuredly doubt was the intention. McCabe's introduction doesn't consider this, nor does he quantify his superlatives. He calls Charles Conlon "the greatest

---

Johnny Evers in both 1904 and 1929 is as edgy as Norman Bates.

---

baseball photographer who ever lived." Speculation about who is the "greatest" is the lifeblood of being a fan, but what does it mean in terms of being a baseball photographer? Did Conlon take the first baseball photos? The most innovative? The most significant? Is a picture of Babe Ruth more important than a picture of Willie Mays? Did Conlon define a style of baseball photography? What makes one photograph better than another? None of this is considered.

The captions place the subjects in baseball history and are well written, although if you are familiar with baseball history, much is familiar. When McCabe quotes contemporary sources, or mentions the circumstances of the photo-taking, the captions are wonderful.

Conlon took the legendary 1909 photo of Ty Cobb sliding into Jimmy Austin at third; however, being concerned about the health of Austin (whom Cobb sent sprawling), Conlon thought he missed the shot, only to discover later he had clicked the shutter out of habit. This is marvelous, but McCabe says the photo "is the greatest baseball action picture ever taken." Again, I want to know why. Because it's one of the few of Cobb in action? Because it's the first baseball action photo? Because it's a unique window on the past? I'm willing to consider all of these, and the photo is certainly one of the most famous. But this isn't the beer commercial. I want to ask why.

The purpose of "Baseball's Golden Age" is to display Charles Conlon's photos, not its text, and the book doesn't claim to be a history of baseball photography. My curiosity was piqued because the photographs are so good and the book looks so good. Many photos I had assumed were just "baseball history" turn out to have been taken by Conlon. The Cobb-Austin shot is the most famous action photo of Cobb. The familiar big-bellied 1910 Cy Young: old, savvy, determined — at the end of the line, but what a line! That was Conlon. The sequence of Hughie Jennings giving his famous "Ee-yaah!" cheer as

Tiger third base coach is Conlon. Last year a picture was offered for sale of a Walter Johnson-Nolan Ryan "dream meeting." It's cribbed and altered from a Conlon photo of Johnson and Lou Gehrig. Photos of Babe Ruth, John McGraw, Mathewson, Wagner and Cobb all look familiar because they are. We've seen Charles Conlon's work for years and not known who he was.

A nice feature are the portraits of the young players next to images of their older selves. Paul Waner is a smooth-faced kid with a bat in 1927; fifteen years later he looks used up. Walter Johnson in 1914 looks remarkably the same in 1935 — strong, serious, self-contained. Johnny Evers in both 1904 and 1929 is as edgy as Norman Bates. Leo Durocher gains a happy shrewdness between 1925 and 1937. Casey Stengel is sharp-eyed and intense in 1924; by '38 that sage face is full of intelligence and humor. Lefty Grove looks similar in 1925 and 1937.

McCabe occasionally sees a man's reputation where I don't. He says Grove in 1925 is glaring "menacingly" at Conlon; Grove just looks country to me. Wes Ferrell is similarly described as "smoldering and ready to explode" in a 1929 photo; to me he looks less "ready to explode" than Dizzy Dean on the opposite page, who, like many of these subjects, looks like a wary redneck.

Another delight of "Baseball's Golden Age" is players whose names are familiar, but whose faces aren't. Here's Jack Graney, the first

---

There's happiness on the face of the old Grover Alexander, which is nice...

---

ex-player to be a radio commentator; Bubbles Hargrave, one of only two catchers to win a batting title; Orval Overall, the other Bill Lee, a swarthy Johnny Kling, a cautious Bill Bergen (his low batting average and taste for high living are mentioned, not his Boston Beaneater brother who killed his family and self one New England winter), a nasty-looking Fielder Jones, and clear-eyed Jake Daubert.

There are two players we have seen but not so clearly. Two fine pictures of Moe Berg show a dark intelligent face, and a 1929 image of Carl Hubbell is one of the most interesting player photos I've seen — there are fear and puzzlement in a face that isn't hidden behind the long mask King Carl seemed to wear later. A shot of Ted Williams

taken on the day of his first big league game shows pain; there's happiness on the face of the old Grover Cleveland Alexander, which is nice considering his difficult post-baseball life; a '29 shot of Connie Mack, dapperly waving his scorecard on the steps of the dugout is exactly the image Mr. Mack wanted to convey; Chick Hafey and Lee Meadows look vulnerable in their glasses; umpires look natty; Joe DiMaggio finishing that mighty swing in 1936 looks lonely. These images have never looked better.

Both the introduction and the last caption end with the phrase "fields of dreams." This is the reigning cliche of our era — and like the movie of the same name, makes baseball simple, sentimental and saleable. Charles Conlon's photographs, like those of Walker Evans or Dorothea Lange, are not simple or sentimental. Conlon doesn't give us a cornfield of nostalgia. He shows us people with their pain, confidence, public faces, tired eyes, intelligence, and he shows it with great art.

LUKE SALISBURY is the author of "The Answer is Baseball" and the novel "The Cleveland Indian."

Coulda Made Us Proud

By David Nemec

W**ITH NOT A WHOLE** lot more attention to detail this might have been the publishing coup of last season — the perfect Christmas gift, arriving as it did in October, for any fan with an ounce of curiosity about the genealogy of his favorite team. Certainly writing a franchise history of even the current 28 teams is a mammoth undertaking. Shooting to nail all 121 clubs that have been members of the six leagues that have gained major league status would unquestionably demand as much bravery as ambition, and Donald Dewey and Nicholas Acocella have plenty of both.

They begin well, too, announcing they have created separate entries for teams that have changed cities. Their logic: any who contend "the Brooklyn Dodgers-Los Angeles Dodgers or Seattle Pilots-Milwaukee Brewers constitute the same franchise" simply have "not talked to a native of Brooklyn or Seattle." And fittingly enough, their alphabetical arrangement of teams allows them a leisurely start with Altoona, the smallest city in major league history and one of the most short-lived.

THE ENCYCLOPEDIA OF MAJOR LEAGUE TEAMS
By Donald Dewey
and Nicholas Acocella
HarperCollins, 1993, 594 pp., $35

Nor do Dewey and Acocella dismiss the Altoona Mountain Citys with a cursory paragraph or two, as previous team histories have been prone to do, because the Altoonians were around for only 25 games and in the most specious of the six major leagues — Henry Lucas's jerry-built Union Association. Instead they provide a cogent report of how the team was formed, why Lucas wooed it, and what factors contributed to its brutally quick demise. Even to readers who know

a bundle about the Mountain Citys, the roles played by tailor James Goetz and hatter Malcolm Westfall in the team's downfall will almost undoubtedly be fresh. Very swiftly Dewey and Acocella establish that theirs will be a groundbreaking work, loaded with anecdotes about characters and teams that were on the scene for scarcely a heartbeat as well as trenchant and unique glimpses into many immortals.

Yet, for all their thought and effort, there is too much lacking in their book for it to stand as an ultimate encyclopedia of major league teams. An encyclopedia is a work encompassing all the various branches of knowledge on a subject, and Dewey and Acocella do indeed imply in their introduction that they will furnish a report for each team balanced between its "feats and failures of the field" and its "executive calculations" and machinations that help us "to understand such apparent anomalies as winning teams (the Oakland Athletics of the 1970s) that created more organizational friction than harmony, losing teams (the New York Mets of the 1960s) that profited from being losers, and profitable teams (the Brooklyn Dodgers of the 1950s) that seized the first opportunity to move elsewhere." But long before I finished it, the introduction planted a suspicion in me that the scale in this book would be tipped heavily toward the executive side of the game.

To test my hunch I looked first at the histories of the New York Giants, Chicago Cubs and Philadelphia Phillies, three teams about equally rich in significant on-field events but markedly different in the style in which they've been run. The New Yorkers, alive for only 74 years (1883-1957) are given 22 pages of text whereas the Cubs, embarking on their 118th season in 1994, get a page less. Phillie fans, knowing their team's history also extends back to 1883, will be upset to discover their team is allotted just 17 pages. The reason is, the Giants, throughout their tenure in New York, had such complex and colorful people at the top as John Day, Andrew Freedman, John McGraw, Bill Terry, Leo Durocher and Charles Stoneham and his son Horace. Baseball's oldest franchise, in contrast, offers Dewey and Acocella few chances to wax on behind-the-scenes chicanery or tumult between the days of Al Spalding and Cap Anson and Durocher's insensitive and impatient hand in the demoralizing late-season collapse of 1969; the Phillies have had no chieftains who can supply the kind of tales that make Andrew Freedman a gold mine for those fascinated by front-office operations.

While visiting the Phillies, I

decided to test Dewey and Acocella on the franchise's most difficult player to evaluate, Chuck Klein. Alas, they take the easy road, embracing the party line on the evidence that he was just a "Baker Bowl hitter." Neither in the Phil or Cub report is there mention of the leg injury that hobbled Klein in 1934 and cut into his power numbers far more than park factors or the challenge of playing with a noncontender. Worse, Dewey and Acocella are guilty of not doing their homework in building their case on Klein. In 1936, after he was traded back to the Phillies, they note that he "hit more round trippers than he had either year in Wrigley Field." Though it's true that Klein's 25 homers that year were his top figure since 1933, his last year with the Phils before being sent westward, only 20 of the 25 were hit after his return to Philadelphia, exactly the same number that he totaled for the Cubs in 1934 and one less than he racked up in 1935.

Lest it might seem I'm being niggling on this point, there are several other junctures in the Phillie report that suggest that Dewey and Acocella's book is not one you should use when you study for a SABR trivia contest. On page 415 they inform us that Charlie Buffinton led the American Association in 1891 with 28 wins; three pages later, in a filler fact, we learn that the Phillies and Giants in 1911 became the "first teams to use different home and away uniforms."

The truth of the matter is that Buffinton's teammate on the Boston Reds, George Haddock, was the Association win leader in 1891 and teams began using different home and away uniforms as far back as the early 1880s.

More in a moment on this trouble Dewey and Acocella have with figures, but first let's get back to the New York Giants, which is in many ways their centerpiece report. Though it is one of the longest and most thorough in the book — fully as long as the report on the much more successful New York Yankees — it nonetheless points up the biggest weakness of this book. Not only does it tend to shortchange on-field events, but in too many instances it is downright stingy. No one, not even in a 200-page book, could be expected to hit all the high spots in every team history. In

the Giant report, though, we are told nothing — not a word — about the agonizingly tight 1899 pennant race that culminated in a Giant victory at the wire, let alone the World Series triumph that fall in what was arguably the stormiest and most interesting postseason in the last century. Dewey and Acocella prefer to dwell on John Day's battle that year to find a new site for a ballpark.

Granted, Klein and the 19th century are special interests of mine and areas where I'm apt to find something to quibble about, so I looked ahead to see how Dewey and Acocella handled the Miracle of Coogan's Bluff and was pleasantly proven wrong for the moment. Their summation of the Giants 1951 season climaxing in "The Shot Heard 'Round the World" is solid, indicating that they can do the job on the field, too, when they care enough.

Still more than willing to give the authors the benefit of the doubt, I tried them again on the Phillies. Now what would you consider the most important moment in Phil history? I can't imagine any bigger than these: 1)Robin Roberts' gutty 4-1 win over Brooklyn in the final game of the 1950 season, bringing the Phils their first pennant in 35 years, and 2)the 1980

postseason that involved the Phils in possibly the most exciting LCS ever, followed by their one and only world championship.

The first was a 1-1 tie at Ebbets Field in the bottom of the tenth. Here's where Dewey and Acocella pick up the action:

"With...Dodger runners on second and first with none out, Duke Snider singled to center off Roberts. Charging the hit, Ashburn fired a perfect strike to Seminick to nab what would have been the winning run. The play seemed to calm down Roberts, who them proceeded to get the next two batters on easy popups and send the contest into the tenth inning {when Dick Sisler's three-run homer won the pennant for the Phils}."

Now wouldn't you like to know who those two Dodgers were, especially Cal Abrams, the guy who was nailed at the plate? And what about the two Dodgers who popped out in the clutch? But if Dewey and Acocella are parsimonious with names in the Roberts game, at least they dish up a taste of the conflict. The entire 1980 postseason rates only a brief paragraph that cites no specific moments of action.

On the other hand, Dewey and Acocella turn a good crisp paragraph on the triumphant 1974 Dodger season that leads into another nicely wrought bit on Mike Marshall. So there is ample evi-

dence that they can deliver vivid and informative prose about the game on the field when they choose to make the effort. In fairness, too, I should say that allowances will gladly be made by many for their erratic and frequently inaccurate descriptions of players and events because their front-office portraits are consistently strong. With some like Charlie Finley, whom they deem a "blowhard, innovator, petty tyrant and miser," they can be almost painfully savage. But if they seem overly ruthless at times, it is generally because their target well deserves it. Only with a few do they don kid gloves.

Connie Mack, my nominee for the title of the game's most venerated villain, is one who sticks in mind. Their explanation for how Mack, the consummate shoestring operator in the 1910s, got enough dough all of a sudden to assemble his late 1920s A's powerhouse is dreadfully lame and skimpy. "Sharing in the general prosperity of the 1920s, Mack began to buy the players who would push the A's beyond respectability into dominance" tells us zip, but it is all we get. Unhappily, the authors continue to seem shy of being openly critical of Mack until age undeniably caused him to begin losing his grip. Charlie Comiskey is also painted with strokes that are more civil than one

would expect, given the hatchet jobs on Freedman, Finley, George Steinbrenner and Calvin Griffith. Only after the club fell into the hands of Comiskey's son Lou and later his grandson Chuck do Dewey and Acocella really get rocking on the White Sox first family.

But these quarrels are minor. It is the uneven and too often errant reportage on team and individual feats — the staples customarily found in club histories — that in the end does irreparable harm to Dewey and Acocella's otherwise monumental achievement. In some cases they can't altogether be faulted. Too many historians over the years have mistakenly written that the Milwaukee and St. Paul teams that joined the Union Association at the end of the 1884 season replaced Wilmington and Pittsburgh respectively for Dewey and Acocella to avoid the same trap. Only by examining the UA's schedule at the beginning of the season and checking Sporting Life for the time period when the transfers occurred can a researcher now unearth that the reverse was true — St. Paul took on Wilmington's schedule after the Quicksteps quit rather than go on the road for the rest of the season, and Milwaukee, replacing Pittsburgh, got to play all home games.

Less forgivable are the many factual errors that mar the text. Gene Bearden will be stunned to read that he appeared in only one game in the 1948 World Series, and Dino Restelli must doubt his own memory for an instant when Dewey and Acocella report than in 1950 the Pirates "broke spring training with an outfield phenom named Dino Restelli. In the third batting slot ahead of Kiner and Westlake, Restelli...belted two homers off Warren Spahn in his second big league game and clouted nine within the first two weeks of the season."

The sad truth is that Restelli didn't play a single game with Pittsburgh in 1950. Nor did his sensational debut come at the beginning of a season. His noisy arrival occurred in June 1949.

But the filler facts are where Dewey and Acocella are at their absolute worst. When they are not offering information that is trite and dull, they are usually getting it wrong. Sam Thompson was not the first person to collect 200 hits in a season, but only one of four players to break the barrier for the first time in 1887. Billy Shindle does not hold the record for most errors in a season with 115; he shares the inglorious mark of 122 with Herman Long. Dan Driessen was the first National Leaguer to bat in the World Series as a designated hitter,

but not against the Red Sox in 1975. It was against the Yankees a year later. One might wonder too where Dewey and Acocella got the tale that Mike Powers became "baseball's first on-field fatality" after "his crash into a wall in pursuit of a popup."

Actually the authors cover their tracks well by almost never mentioning their sources. One would begin to assume automatically that they knew whereof they wrote in their intriguing vignette on Watch Burnam, manager of the Indianapolis Hoosiers at the beginning of the 1887 season, were it not for the many gaffes in their reports on 19th century teams, figures and events. The famous "Candlelight game" on September 7, 1889 between Brooklyn and St. Louis did not end abruptly when Charlie Comiskey refused to let his Browns take the field in the ninth inning but after the inning was already underway and the Bridegrooms had a runner on second. Moreover, the crucial series between the two American Association contenders was originally slated to be three games, not just two as Dewey and Acocella claim.

The 19th century jewel in their book is a nifty account of how the American Association was formed that I shall not spoil except to say it should be taken with a barrel of salt. Turning as it does on an aborted meeting in Pittsburgh, I'm curi-

ous what Dewey and Acocella have done with the evidence that the meeting took place. I'd be very ready to concede that the principals involved doctored the evidence by planting false newspaper stories, etc. — they were certainly capable of it — but what then happened to the people like John Day and Chris Von der Ahe who were allegedly at the meeting? Can anyone really imagine that Day or Von der Ahe would not have seen the newspaper reports of the session? This was October 1881 in America, after all, not 1581 when communication between areas was still delivered mostly via smoke signals. And if either Von der Ahe or Day had gotten wind of the meeting they reputedly attended, how probable is it that they would have fallen for a ruse that depended on their believing that they alone among important invitees had not been there?

And amazingly, despite the likelihood that Dewey and Acocella either overlooked or ignored all the available evidence in forming their theory, it is still probably closer to the truth than anything else about the AA's birth that's ever been published by a major house.

Now that the silent partner in Dewey and Acocella's endeavor has been put on the table, let me go on awhile about my biggest grievance with this book.

It is usually wrongheaded to hold a book's shortcomings against a publisher. An author — in this case, plural — is responsible for doing the necessary research, choosing where his emphasis will lie, and doublechecking himself to be absolutely sure that enough of

> ## Dewey and Acocella are always entertaining even when they verge on being exasperating.

the existing evidence will support him when he goes out on a limb. When two authors collaborate, as these have, on a monstrous project, it's never possible to assess who did what. Was it Dewey or Acocella who dug up all the great stuff on obscure owners while Acocella or Dewey was butchering material that is taught in Baseball 101? Or did they share equally in their triumphs and pratfalls? I haven't a clue. But I do know that a decent reader, using only The Macmillan Encyclopedia and Total Baseball as references, could have spared them many of their errors. Maybe Dewey and Acocella were unlucky and were given an editor who usually works

on cookbooks. Again, I have no way of knowing. But I don't think that I'm being cruel in saying that although they ought to have pushed for a sharper reader or else found one on their own, they were not given much help by their publisher. In addition to far too many lapses in the text is the omission of an index. We could really profit from one in a book of this length and density. I think most readers will find too that the paucity of photographs — and many of them Hall of Fame plaques at that — further suggests that the publisher cut corners to keep the price of the book down. It was an unfortunate decision. Another $5 might have made all the difference, for Dewey and Acocella are always entertaining even when they verge on being exasperating. Though the on-field omissions and basic errors are too numerous to qualify The Encyclopedia of Major League Teams as the definitive work on the subject, Dewey and Acocella made a valiant try at the crown. That they fell short is disappointing but will at the same time be encouraging to some out there. The door is still open for the next heavyweight contender who cares enough and is daring enough to wade into the task of telling 121 separate but interwoven tales.

DAVID NEMEC has written "The Great American Baseball Team Book," "Great Baseball Feats, Facts, and Firsts," and "The Rules of Baseball." He is currently working on "The Beer and Whisky League," a pictorial history of the American Association, to be published this fall by Lyons & Burford.

The Passion of the Purist

By Andrew Milner

BILL MEISSNER IS A BASE-ball purist, and damn proud of it. At a time when sincere appreciation of the game is scoffed at and considered as passe as button shoes and LPs, Meissner has offered "Hitting into the Wind," a lyrical, accessible, and above all relevant collection of baseball short stories. Although by no means perfect, its occasional lapses are more than mitigated by Meissner's overall precision cum passion.

The passion for baseball in these back-to-basic stories is found within the game's basic elements. Meissner's characters savor the caps, the gloves, the baseballs themselves. The protagonist of one story rescues the horsehides from abandoned fields while in another ("The Unwinding") a father watches his young son unravel a baseball just to see what's inside.

HITTING INTO THE WIND
By Bill Meissner
Random House, 1994, 224 pp., $18

Another story is devoted to "The Glove Lacers": "They connect the glove to itself, which in turn connects to the hand of the player, which in turn connects to the ball." Likewise, the practicality of these artifacts — you can hold them in your hand, put them in your pocket — underscores the intimate way they connect people to the Game.

As Meissner writes about the Game on a simple level, those real-life players he celebrates are not the Adonises but those players who overcome. In "A Song for Hank Aaron's Swing," Meissner recalls one of Henry's 755:

Once, in Milwaukee County Stadium, I watched you hit what seemed to be an infield pop-up down the third base line. The ball climbed the air and didn't stop until, far

beyond the outfield fence, it poked a hole through the glass floor of heaven...That homer was you, Henry, rising so modestly, pushing your shoulders against the heavy sky that tried to hold you down.

"Kirby Puckett's Legs: A Symphony in Nine Innings" shows how average fans connect to the Twin star of ordinary build who performs the extraordinary.

The score's tied in the ninth, and for a moment it looks like Kirby's running in place. But no. He's merely accelerating. Kirby Puckett's legs: thumping turkey drumsticks, adrenalized heartbeats.

What saves Meissner's prose from preciousness is the underlying recognition that it's dangerous to confuse the realities of the diamond for those of day-to-day existence (or, as Spy Magazine once noted, to see "life as a metaphor for baseball"). In Meissner's neighborhood a field of dreams can all too easily become a field of delusions.

Darwin, the thirtysomething husband in "What About the World," prefers batting practice to acknowledging the deterioration of his marriage, assuredly telling himself in Kinsella-esque language, "When I walk away from that field after a couple hours of baseball, I'm a better person. I can face the world...I'm playing ball, and I'm stopping death, right there on that little sandlot field." Sadly, Darwin's passion for the game has not evolved into similar feelings for those who love him.

Meissner draws upon this same conflict in "Things Are Always So Close." Roger, an amateur umpire, must go beyond the simple ball-strike, safe-out calls to render a judgment when he thinks his wife's been unfaithful.

He could never get his emotions in line so he could explain them, not to anyone, not even to himself...If he was at a ball game, and he had a logical argument, he could raise his voice in a controlled way like he did with any barking manager or fuming player after a close play. He could raise his voice and say just what was needed...But this was different. He stood there, facing the layer of wood in the darkness, knowing he didn't understand her at all, and he simply didn't know what to say.

This story in particular displays Meissner's skills; when was the last time a fiction writer made you empathize with an umpire?

Meissner's take on baseball is so

original and honest that it's a pity he relies on cliche in his weaker stories. The title of "The John F. Kennedy Wiffle Ball" is self-explanatory; a young boy in the early '60s names his perforated plastic baseball after the 35th president, and everything is ruddy until November 22, 1963. Using JFK's assassination as a metaphor for loss of personal or generational innocence is not exactly an original pop culture device, and I was disappointed Meissner had nothing really new to say about the trauma.

The Joe DiMaggio-Marilyn Monroe saga has proven irresistible to the best writers, but Meissner's ambitious "Lights: Joe and Marilyn, an American Love Story" doesn't quite come off. Especially embarrassing is Meissner's description of the effect the couple's divorce had upon the country.

> When the marriage ended, America...saw that something had changed. Maybe the storybook's final pages were torn out, the edges suddenly jagged and rough. Maybe the world wasn't all Victory and love and sweethearts and smiles. For the first time America realized that maybe not everything was going to last, maybe there'd be losses that no one expected.

That's a bit much. Most Americans of that era unexpectedly lost a lot: the Depression, World War II, the Korean War, McCarthyism. Joe and Marilyn's breakup was seismic, but to 1954 America it was more likely the last straw, not the first.

On the whole, Meissner's stories resonate with the sound of confident, unforced writing meeting equally strong subject matter. The better stories (among them, "What About the World," "Kirby Puckett's Legs," and "The Man Who Rescued Baseballs") can transport and surprise, much as the game does at its best.

Bill Meissner is an author who understands that baseball exists as much in the mind as it does on the field, and that understated writing is enough; just present the dots, and let the readers connect them. "Hitting into the Wind" proves you don't need expanded playoffs or haphazard postseason TV coverage (or a November World Series) to care deeply and truly about baseball.

ANDREW MILNER, graduate of Syracuse University, has contributed to this publication and "The SABR Review of Books." He wrote his senior thesis on the influence of the Black Sox Scandal on modern American fiction.

Look and See

By Frederick Ivor-Campbell

WHEN KEITH HER-nandez was a boy, his father, "a former minor leaguer who believed that sloppy baseball was a serious sin," not only drilled him and his brother Gary on the fundamentals of the game "for hours on end," but gave them *written tests*. We're not told how Gary responded to this intense training (did he become an opera singer?) but we know how Keith turned out — a premier first baseman and one of the most astute observers of the game. Now it's his turn to educate us. In "Pure Baseball," his second collaboration with Mike Bryan (a fine writer, and, as his solo books demonstrate, also an astute observer and keen analyst), Hernandez instructs us in viewing the game. "Pure Baseball," which closely studies a pair of June 1993 contests, is our textbook, "a guide

PURE BASEBALL:
Pitch by Pitch for the Advanced Fan
By Keith Hernandez and Mike Bryan
HarperCollins, 1994, 259 pp., $21

to anticipating the plays, watching the action, and judging the strategy in any game [we] attend."

In the first half of the book Hernandez guides us through an Atlanta loss at Philadelphia, which he attended as a spectator, and in the second half we study a 10-inning Detroit loss at New York, which Hernandez watched on TV with the sound turned off. (A further indication of his intelligence.)

As the book's subtitle suggests, Hernandez' chief interest is the contest between pitcher and batter. "For me," he writes, "this battle of wits and balance of talent between the pitcher and the hitter is baseball. Everything else is secondary." Maybe so, but pitches laid out in black on white make for a slow read, even though we aren't required to ponder literally *every* pitch.

To be fair, Hernandez does give us more than a mere pitch-by-pitch, play-by-play examination of the two games. His father's son, he drills us on the fundamentals, and provides numerous asides —

> **Should enough fans and players sign up for this course of study with Prof Hernandez, we might see a return to the good old days.**

sometimes pages long — to discuss general points of strategy. Frequently, too, he assesses the styles of play not only of participants in these two games but also of other players he himself played with and against in his long career. He is not shy about challenging the conventional wisdom. He is convinced, for example, that it isn't difficult for a batter to pull an outside pitch. He also willingly hands out advice to particular players. For one, now that Wade Boggs is a Yankee, he should adjust to pull the ball more to Yan-kee Stadium's short right field.

Boggs, though, resembles Ted Williams in refusing to alter a style that has worked well for him, and when he ironically does homer to right to win the Yankee-Tiger contest in the tenth inning, Hernandez quotes the third baseman's postgame interview complaint that "this at bat was all a mistake, that he got out in front of the pitch."

I've called "Pure Baseball" a textbook, and while we can read it from start to finish the way we read a novel, or a biography, or a team history, we might enjoy it more, and profit more from it, if we read it the way teachers urged us to read our textbooks when we were in school: not all at once the night before the final exam, but a chapter at a time, with reflection between chapters. "Pure Baseball" doesn't follow its chapters with discussion questions, but we might do well to read it as though it did, and pause every so often to review what we've learned, and maybe think of further examples from games we've played in or watched ourselves.

While the book is directed toward "the advanced fan," much of what Hernandez explains might be old hat to the truly knowledgeable spectator. Its target audience might be more accurately described as the "advanced fan wannabe."

Perhaps more importantly, the book might be just as valuable to the advanced *player*. It is not an

instructional in the ordinary sense: no photos or diagrams, except for elaborate scorecards of the two games. But I can imagine high school and college coaches, and maybe even professional managers, assigning "Pure Baseball" as part of spring training, a chapter a day, followed by group discussion.

One welcome feature of the book is its index, with references not only to players but to plays. Under "base runners," for example, we find the subhead "smart," which points us to a page describing Jeff Blauser's intelligent baserunning in the Phils-Braves game. The index has the added value of making the book usable as a reference work, although it could be improved and expanded. Jim Eisenreich's heady baserunning is listed only under his name and the subhead "as base runner." And why not a "base runners" subhead of "dumb" that targets Spike Owen's blunder which ends a Yankee threat in the seventh?

It's a common complaint of old-timers that most players today don't discuss the game on the field in the detailed and wholly absorbed way they used to. Neither do most spectators. (These days our most intense discussions seem to be about stats.) Should enough fans and players sign up for this course of study with Professor Hernandez, though, we might see a return to the good old days, maybe even a new golden age of baseball.

FREDERICK IVOR-CAMPBELL is a baseball historian.

The Baseball Fiction Hall of Fame:

Preliminaries

Compiled by Paul Adomites

Contributors: Peter Carino, Gene Carney, Pete Cava, Jim Distelhorst, Richard Gaughran, Jack Kavanagh, Nancy Jo Leachman, Stephen Lehman, Andy McCue, Andrew Milner, Jim O'Donnell, Bobby Plapinger, Luke Salisbury, Mark Schraf, Clifford Wexler.

ONE OF THE MOST SUCCESSFUL pieces in THE REVIEW (although in its previous incarnation as "The SABR Review of Books") was "The Essential Baseball Library," in which we surveyed a panel of experts to determine which baseball books no self-respecting expert could possibly do without. Now we're doing the same for baseball fiction. The members of the panel all have remarkable credentials for tackling this chore, and as we expected, they responded in glorious fashion: intelligent, opinionated, insightful and rude — all the things we want from our critics.

Our plan is to create a true "Baseball Fiction Hall of Fame," which

is where all our readers come in. Check out this "preliminary" article and let us know what you think of the opinions voiced here. Where there is true consensus, we will make appropriate decisions and announce the first entries into "The Hall" in next year's issue. The readers of this publication are the most literate baseball fans in the world, so we suspect any author receiving "Hall" status will be respectful of the high honor it represents.

The participants in this survey were asked to select their choices for the top nine works of baseball fiction of all time, annotate their lists, and then mention any other works they felt deserved comment, good or bad. All in all 60 books were mentioned by the 14 panelists; 19 were listed only in "the second string" category.

Then we asked, "How do you define a baseball novel?" Plenty of books have baseball references; plenty have the Game as a background. Does a baseball novel have to have on-field action, or are references to the Game enough? Here's what they said.

What Defines A Baseball Novel?

On this subject (unlike others) the panel largely agreed on a basic concept: that to be a "baseball novel" the baseball in the book has to be essential to the book. If the role baseball played could have been taken by the film industry, or soccer, the novel doesn't pass the test. Clifford Wexler put it this way: "A baseball novel uses baseball as the field upon which the narrative plays itself out. On or off the field, in the dugout or the executive suite, in the mind or in the heart, baseball must be at the center of the novel. [And] the novel must be true to the game."

Mark Schraf said the judgment had to be made on whether the book "Has to do with the magic of the game...baseball must make a difference, an impact, on the lives written about." More than one panelist agreed with Nancy Jo Leachman, who said, "If you have to ask, the answer is no." But Andrew Milner took it an intriguing step

further: "[In a true baseball novel] the conflict is between those characters who love and enjoy the game on an innocent level, and those
who would simply exploit the sport."

The Rankings

Although many members of the panel preferred not to rank their
choices within the top nine, of those who did, only four books were
felt deserving of the handle "Best of All Time": Four panel members
listed Robert Coover's "The Universal Baseball Association, J. Henry
Waugh, Prop.," as the best. Two chose Mark Harris's "The Southpaw," and one Harris's "Bang the Drum Slowly." Bernard Malamud's
"The Natural" also received one "best" ranking. If we apply a somewhat arbitrary point system (10 points for being named "Best Baseball Novel Ever," 5 for each mention in the top nine, and 1 for mention in the second string, seven novels clearly outdistance the pack.
In order of points:

1. "The Universal Baseball Association, J. Henry Waugh, Prop."
by Robert Coover.
2. "The Celebrant," by Eric Rolfe Greenberg.
3. "The Natural," by Bernard Malamud.
4. "The Southpaw," by Mark Harris.
5. "You Know Me, Al," by Ring Lardner.
6. "Shoeless Joe," by W.P. Kinsella.
7. "Bang the Drum Slowly," by Mark Harris.

It was only the four votes for "all-time best" that kept Coover's
work in front of Greenberg's. "The Celebrant" was ranked among the
top nine baseball novels of all time by *thirteen of the fourteen* panel
members.

Here are comments on "The Celebrant." Schraf: "It's what it
means to be a fan." Milner: "In all likelihood the best baseball novel
of them all. This works on so many levels." McCue: "An immensely
powerful novel examining heroism and obsession." O'Donnell:
"Christ symbols abound in a well-crafted novel that could just as
aptly be called 'Jews for Christy.'" On the somewhat troubling subject

of the novel's religious allusions, Bob Plapinger commented, "I just ignored that part."

Coover's novel brought out some fascinating concepts on the part of the panelists. Luke Salisbury feels that "UBA" is far and away the best baseball novel ever. He says, "Baseball fiction is 'Ernie Banks and eight other guys.'" Jim Distelhorst seemed to agree: "The ultimate baseball book — although it contains no real baseball at all!" Mark Schraf talked about the "incredibly vibrant depiction of the strength of 'the inner game of baseball' (the one in our mind's eye)." Milner: "I always thought Waugh went a bit far myself. Until I joined a Fantasy League." Leachman: "Coover can write. But I have never been able to forgive Henry for not caring about the game of baseball itself."

Jim O'Donnell calls Coover's book "The preeminent baseball novel. No other writer has explored as effectually...the seductive danger in baseball's hold on the imagination."

Lehman: "Baseball fan as God; God as an Obsessive-Compulsive...Why not? after all, 'In the Big Inning was the Word...'" Gaughran: "A novel about a game that tries to replicate a game, but mostly an important examination of the need to control, and when necessary to revise, the 'fictions' by which we all live."

"The Natural" is a work that appears on most lists, yet many panelists noted they had included it because of its historical importance as the first "literary" baseball novel. The comments were not universally praiseworthy. Wexler: "Captures the essence of the game as we would like to imagine it, in a perfect blending of form and style." Milner: "It has the universal issues of guilt and human fallibility that Malamud focused on in subsequent fiction." Cava: "The ultimate baseball novel, cleverly intertwining classic mythology with baseball legend." Carino: "Taken as the dark myth it is, this is a wonderful book."

But Gaughran feels it is "weighed down by mythic correspondences." Schraf: "Although flawed in many places...Malamud explores 'baseball as mythology' with elan." Salisbury: "It works as the deep male fantasy of the envious, deadly, random femme fatale we secretly fear hunts our balls —but I never liked the baseball." Andy McCue felt "The Natural" missed the point altogether. "It

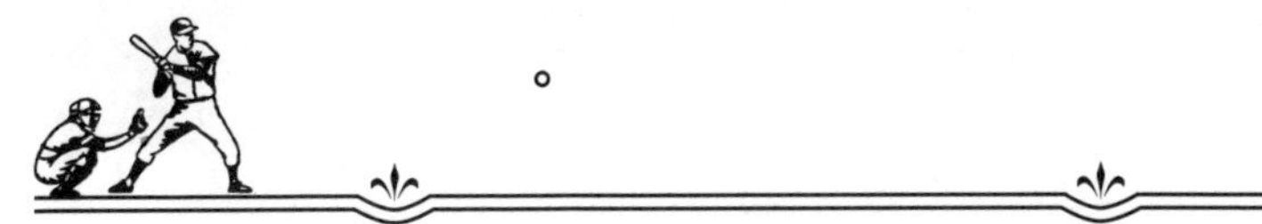

brings that real overblown, Armageddonish football mentality to baseball. It's too bad that Malamud's great books weren't about baseball."

Two authors appeared most often: Mark Harris and W.P. Kinsella. Jim O'Donnell created a special category of "Sustained Achievement" for those two, Philip Roth and Ring Lardner.

Although Kinsella was most often mentioned for "Shoeless Joe," with his other works frequently considered secondary, Harris, on the other hand, placed two novels ("The Southpaw" and "Bang the Drum Slowly)" in the Big Seven, and received top-nine votes for "It Looked Like Forever," and "A Ticket for a Seamstitch" as well. Bob Plapinger said, "I can't choose between 'em." Andy McCue said "I'm happy to have any of the Wiggen books at the top of the list," adding, "In Wiggen's voice, Harris found a way to bring together baseball's rural roots and its metropolitan present, and to illuminate the society around the game as well as the game itself." Steve Lehman (probably not realizing his opinions were shared by many on the panel) defensively said, "So I like the Henry Wiggen stories. So sue me."

Jim Distelhorst felt that "The Southpaw" is "the best 'coming of age' baseball novel." Mark Schraf liked the way "Bang the Drum Slowly" explores the human psyche. Peter Carino noted that "It Looked Like Forever" is "An excellent chronicle of a skilled athlete coming to terms with his mortality. It also anticipates much of the prostitution of the game to money and television." Bob Plapinger agreed: "Henry dealing with the end of his career, trying to last one more season..trying to figure out what happens next."

The oldest fiction to make the list, Ring Lardner's work, particularly "You Know Me Al," "set the direction for much baseball fiction that followed," according to Clifford Wexler. Jim O'Donnell thinks the achievement is even larger: "It established the subgenre of baseball fiction, albeit in a sardonic vein," according to Jim O'Donnell. Jack Kavanagh stated unequivocally, "This is the funniest baseball book." Andrew Milner noted that "this novel clearly establishes that

the Chicago White Sox had already caught America's literary fancy before 1919...In Jack Keefe, Lardner created the stereotype — we pretty much retain it today — of the innocent rookie called up to the Big Show." Pete Cava underscores that idea: "Those who know Lardner's stories and who have listened to interviews on ESPN's SportsCenter know that Jack's spiritual descendants are alive and well, and wearing big league uniforms."

If points had been distributed for the total works of a single author, W.P. Kinsella would have led all others. "Shoeless Joe" tied "UBA," "The Natural," and "You Know Me, Al" with nine mentions in the top nine (behind only "The Celebrant"). Kinsella also received top-tier votes for "The Iowa Baseball Confederacy" and "The Thrill of the Grass," a collection of short stories. Andy McCue prefers Kinsella's short fiction to his novels.

Richard Gaughran feels that "Shoeless Joe" is "probably responsible for igniting what seems to be the baseball fiction explosion of the last ten or twelve years."

Six panelists felt the need to comment on the sentimentality of "Shoeless Joe," but few felt it got in the way. Peter Carino said "at times it gets downright hokey, [but] it spins a good yarn and is beautifully written." Jack Kavanagh referred to it as "a bit cutesy and pretentious — but it comes off!" Mark Schraf: "I don't find this novel saccharine."

Nancy Jo Leachman has a personal stake in the book. "I 'discovered' 'Shoeless Joe' immediately following its publication and instantly felt I had a personal stake in the book. As its literary fame spread and then its rebirth due to the movie, I became distressed. I didn't want to share it — I suspected very few people out there were as worthy of this book as I. Such a spiritual book shouldn't be allowed to become desecrated by being popular with the masses. How thoughtless of Kinsella to let everybody else read it, too."

But the panel was far from unanimous. Luke Salisbury had strong feelings: "'Shoeless Joe' blazed an economic trail for baseball fiction, and did it the old fashioned away: trivialize, sentimentalize, and sell.

Schmaltz it and they will come... 'Shoeless Joe' is certainly one of the nine most important baseball novels. It tells us too much about what too many of us really want."

Steve Lehman listed "Shoeless Joe," but added, "Almost disqualified because of the embarrassing Salinger peroration on how baseball harkens back to a time of innocence and goodness and motherhood and moral purity. So do diapers, but that doesn't mean we sentimentalize incontinence. It was worse having a black man say it in the movie. How come Satchel and Josh and Mule and Oscar, et al., weren't invited to the Field of Dreams, hmmm?"

[Speaking of films, there was no agreement among the panel about the quality of the films made from the novels on the list.]

Harry Stein's "Hoopla" received four votes for the top nine, but there was disagreement on whether it or Brendan Boyd's "Blue Ruin" was the better Black Sox novel.

The only other novel to receive more than three votes for ranking among the top nine is a surprise. Douglass Wallop's 1954 fantasy "The Year the Yankees Won the Pennant." Luke Salisbury calls this "the title of the decade, along with 'Rock Around the Clock.'" This editor, for one, plans to dust that one off and read it again. Especially since Andrew Milner has identified several unsettling links to the Hardy Boys young detective series.

Several other works were rated highly enough by our panel to appear in the top nine rankings of three of them. Darryl Brock's "If I Never Get Back" (of which Pete Cava says, "Brock has contemplated a sequel... I can't wait"), Philip Roth's "Great American Novel" (which Andrew Milner called "side-splittingly hilarious, in small doses"), and panelist Luke Salisbury's "The Cleveland Indian," which Peter Carino noted was "in the tradition of classic American novels through a plot linking a white Protestant male and a non-white hero."

Martin Quigley, author of the highly respected non-fiction work "The Crooked Pitch," received mention for two of his novels, "The Original Colored House of David" and "Today's Game."

Although the survey didn't ask about them, books for young readers were also called out for special notice by several panelists. Nancy Leachman talked about "Baseball Saved Us," by Ken Mochizuki with illustrations by Dom Lee. The tale of baseball in the Japanese-American internments camps during World War II, it was selected as one of best children's books of the past year. As Nancy says, "It's a moving story, well told and beautiful illustrated; it's a story of baseball as a great equalizer; it educates on an unfortunately neglected part of our history…and there are no others anything like it."

Andy McCue said of John R. Tunis, "I think this list must recognize the powerful place in our lives occupied by the baseball fiction we read as children. It helped form the picture frame through which we viewed the game and measured what actions within it were appropriate."

And again, even though the question wasn't asked, several panelists mentioned baseball mysteries: Jim Distelhorst chose Loren D. Estleman's "King of the Corner" as best ever. Nancy Jo Leachman preferred "Strike Three You're Dead" by Richard Rosen. She explains "It's the best because baseball knowledge truly does play a part in figuring the motive. A fan will figure it out before a non-fan."

Other interesting comments about multiple vote-getters. Andrew Milner on Jerome Charyn's "The Seventh Babe": "One great modern baseball novel you almost never hear anything about. "

Richard Gaughran on Dom DeLillo's novella "Pafko at the Wall": "A major voice in contemporary American literature fictionalizes arguably the most dramatic moment in baseball history — with J. Edgar Hoover, Jackie Gleason, Frank Sinatra, the Cold War, and an awestruck but resourceful boy!" Of Peter Lefcourt's "The Dreyfus Affair," Nancy Jo Leachman said, "If it weren't against my creed to be judgmental, I'd say baseball needed this book."

Books which received more than one vote for the top tier included "The Brothers K" by David James Duncan, "Prospect" by Bill Littlefield (of which Jack Kavanagh says: "It'll make a fine movie — will someone please discover this?"), John Hough's "The Conduct of

the Game," and Damon Rice's "Seasons Past." Michael Shaara (author of "The Killer Angels," the basis for the film "Gettysburg") received two mentions for "For the Love of the Game," as did Donald Hayes' "The Dixie Association" and Jane Leavy's "Squeeze Play."

Several books received no front runner votes, but were mentioned often in the second tier: James Brashler's "Bingo Long" and Barbara Gregorich's "She's On First" were listed five times each. Among works of short fiction, four books of short stories, both by individuals and compilations, received votes: Jerry Klinkowitz's "Short Season," Bill Meissner's "Hitting into the Wind" (reviewed in this issue), "Baseball and the Game of Life," and "Tales of the Diamond."

And as the last word, leave it to our longtime friend Jack Kavanagh to try and create an all-new subgenre. "Most of the Putnam series [of team histories] seem to be heavily loaded with fiction, too."

Thanks to the panelists for their exceptional work. Now it's time for you to speak up — What books do you think belong in The Baseball Fiction Hall of Fame?

O-for-Transcendence

By Jim Kaplan

REINHOLD NIEBUHR ONCE took his fellow theologian and philosopher, the German-born Paul Tillich, to a baseball game. Hard as he tried, Niebuhr couldn't explain the action to the initiate. Niebuhr waxed technical, philosophical and historical, but to no avail: Tillich was utterly stumped. Finally, the home team made a spectacular double play, and the crowd went wild. Tillich again turned to Niebuhr, wondering how an act that involved no scoring could have evoked such a thunderous response. Niebuhr explained anew; Tillich remained baffled. At this point Niebuhr threw up his arms and exclaimed, "It's a *kairos*, Paulus, it's a *kairos*!"

"Kairos" is Greek for an event so wondrous and transcendent that there must have been divine intervention. Paul Tillich smiled and nodded. He was finally beginning to understand baseball.

I have often cited this anecdote as the ultimate defense of baseball as transcendence, nobility, bliss and other good things generally. Unfortunately, baseball's metaphysical qualities have been taking a pounding of late. From neanderthals emerge viewpoints like the one the Boston Sunday Globe's "Focus" page published before the 1994 season.

With an air of innocence and discovery, the author wondered how writers could rhapsodize over a game played by junkies, adulterers and tax cheats. Of course, you and I know that baseball has always been played by junkies, adulterers and tax cheats -- and has scarcely skipped a poetic beat. And what about all the great literature, music,

---

BASEBALL & THE GAME OF IDEAS:
Essays for the Serious Fan
Edited by Peter C. Bjarkman
Birch Brook Press, 1993, $25

acting and performing by those whose personal resumes are full of bobbles? Do we let that get in the way of a good song or story?

The problem is not the baseball rhapsody. It's the less-than-melodic beat -- overworked, overanalyzed, overblown--of too many literary tributes to our national pastime. I mean, "Baseball & The Game of Ideas: Essays for the Serious Fan"?

What really bothers me is the ampersand.

A subject so abstract needs focus. The Ron Fimrite-edited "Birth of a Fan" (Macmillan, 1993, $22), a collection of essays about growing up with baseball, might have served as a model. Unfortunately, Peter Bjarkman's choices for "Baseball & The Game of Ideas," while enthusiastic and wide-ranging, are ultimately scattershot. They work as well together as trying to ground a jet with bb's.

Occasionally, Bjarkman's selections make contact. "Why No One Hits .400 Any More" by Stephen Jay Gould gives little truck to popular explanations like grueling schedules, jet travel across time zones, night games, the slider, improved fielding and relief pitching. Using data and charts rather than hot air, Gould argues that the decline in standard deviations between "average and stellar play" limits spectacular recordings. "As variation shrinks around a constant mean batting average, .400 hitting disappears...The extinction of .400 hitting is...a mark of increasingly *better* play."

This is a real contribution: the substitution of facts for popular assumption in baseball debate.

There are some other four-bag scripts. "Little League: An Idea Whose Time Has Come...And Gone" by Jay Feldman makes the best attack on organized kids' baseball I've ever read. Mark Harris's "Horatio at the Bat, or Why Such a Lengthy Embryonic Period for the Serious Baseball Novel?" helps our understanding of diamond fiction despite its unwieldy title.

Some writers serve up impressive deliveries of baseball as symbol. In "Baseball and American Manhood" by Merritt Clifton, baseball is described as a fertility rite rather than the coming-of-age macho ritual so many sports represent. "Hunting is about rape, football about immature sexuality; baseball, and baseball alone, goes beyond the rutting stage to teach men to be not only mates but also good husbands, and eventually, good examples for other men."

Some of the other essays are seriously dated. "Baseball and the Urban Crisis" by James Kissane was written in 1968, and didn't tell us much then. "The New Mythopoeism [sic] of Baseball: W.P. Kinsella's Baseball Fiction," by

Thomas L. Altherr, labors through yet another guide to "Field of Dreams" as religious allegory. A couple of dreary stories about Canadian baseball entertained me about as much as drum solos. John B. Holway's "Diamond Stars: Baseball Astrology" and David Q. Voigt's "Thank God for Nuts -- They Flavor the Game," reprint SABR articles from The National Pastime and The Baseball Research Journal, respectively. Essays? Serious? I don't think I'll consult the stars before selecting my next fantasy league team. Nor do I need to be reminded that Yogi was funny.

How could Bjarkman have failed to include an essay on the business of baseball, the one subject above all else demanding serious interpretation? Bjarkman whiffs again in a text-ending compilation of "all-star" articles, essays, non-fiction books, biographies, historical volumes and number-crunching works. There are fully five different listings under Bjarkman himself. He includes "Mitts" by Bill Curran while omitting a far superior book on fielding, "Nine Sides of the Diamond" by David Falkner. Fortunately, one of the book's contributions, "The Minoans -- A Whole New Ballgame" by John S. Bowman, gives the weary reader some welcome relief. Perfectly deadpan, Bowman takes the Phaestos Disc and documents how one side contained "Take Me Out to the Ballgame" and the other side "Casey at the Bat." Bowman's work parodies both archaeological and baseball research and debate.

In "Baseball & The Game of Ideas," only the Minoan text could truly be described as a *kairos*.

JIM KAPLAN, a freelance writer who formerly wrote for Sports Illustrated and edited The Baseball Research Journal, was described by George Will as "the poet laureate of fielding." Kaplan's most recent baseball book, co-authored by New York Times columnist Ira Berkow, is "The Gospel According to Casey: Casey Stengel's Inimitable, Instructional, Historical Baseball Book" (St. Martin's Press).

Matty the Magnificent

By Jerry Tomlinson

WHEN CHRISTY Mathewson died at Saranac Lake, New York, at the age of forty-five, Baseball Commissioner Kenesaw Mountain Landis, never a sentimentalist, asked, "Why should God wish to take a thoroughbred like Matty so soon, and leave some others down here that could well be spared?" Yes, Matty was a thoroughbred. The handsome master of the fadeaway and America's greatest baseball idol prior to Babe Ruth surely deserves a first-rate biography.

Ray Robinson's "Matty: An American Hero" may or may not be that biography, depending on your expectations. The baseball history in the book is neatly and colorfully presented. Robinson devotes a good deal of space, as you might expect, to the 1905 World Series and Matty's all-but-incredible and almost certainly unmatchable three shutouts. He also covers in suitable detail the exciting (if ultimately unhappy for Giant fans) 1908 season, in which Big Six won 37 games while losing 11, posting a 1.43 ERA. Which was not his best single- season ERA at that — he topped it two other times.

The author's play-by-play reporting, never dull, moves the Matty story along with verve, and the nonbaseball events of the early twentieth century, sharply encapsulated by Robinson, help to put the game in historical perspective. It's a pleasant mix, and it works. An occasional anachronism is hardly fatal, as, for instance, when Matty and his bride move to "Baghdad on the Subway" in 1901. (Robinson is borrowing a short-story title from O. Henry). New York City would

---

MATTY: AN AMERICAN HERO
By Ray Robinson
Oxford University Press, 1993,
236 pp., $23

merit the sobriquet very soon — the first subway was built three years later. But in 1901, before O. Henry's own arrival in the city, it was still Baghdad on the El. A bit more serious is Robinson's error of ascribing the 1914 assassination of Austrian Archduke Francis Ferdinand and his wife to "a Bosnian nationalist." Holy Sarajevo! This murderous act, which touched off World War I, or the Great War, as it was then called, was committed by one Gavrilo Princip, a *Serbian* nationalist, and a hero of the Serbs from that day to this. But back to baseball...

Or rather back to Christy Mathewson. He's the subject of the book, after all, or he's supposed to be. Therein lies the problem. For where in these 236 pages of baseball action is the living, breathing Matty? Where is the guy who must have lived a full, variegated life, sometimes exciting, sometimes mundane -- with his wife Jane, his son Christy, Jr., his dog (did he have a dog?), which is to say, a life beyond the inevitable train rides and oft-mentioned checkers matches, a life in which he wasn't forever exercising that famous pinpoint control from the mound for the New York Giants? If Big Six had an existence off the field, it isn't much in evidence here. One season ends, another begins.

It's not that Ray Robinson is incapable of writing a well-rounded biography. He's done it. His "Iron Horse: Lou Gehrig in His Time," published in 1990, is an excellent portrayal of Gehrig's life and times. Naturally, Babe Ruth looms large in the Gehrig story, as he would have to, but he doesn't virtually take it over, as John McGraw sometimes does in "Matty." There are stretches in this book where a browsing reader might conclude that the title ought to be "Mugsy: Manager and Friend." Although indexes are not always a reliable guide to coverage, consider this: The index entry for John McGraw takes up five linear inches, more than is devoted to the whole Mathewson family (the great Christy himself, father Gilbert, brother Henry, wife Jane, son John Christopher, mother Minerva, and brother Nicholas). Little Napoleon scores big. Even his wife Blanche overshadows Jane Mathewson until the scene shifts at last, fatally and sadly, to Saranac Lake.

Robinson's opening chapter makes a case for Mathewson's being "the first authentic [American] sports hero." Without disputing that, I'd have to ask what assumptions lie behind the word "authentic"? There were nineteenth-century baseball idols aplenty. What diminished the "authenticity" of, say, the wildly popular King Kelly? Another writer, Donald Honig, in "The Greatest Pitchers of All

Time," clarifies what I suspect Robinson has in mind: "He [Mathewson] was the first American sports hero whose appeal crossed all social, economic and cultural boundaries." Fair enough. One could view the earlier stars mostly as flawed roustabouts. Matty was perceived as being flawless.

He wasn't, no one is, but he was an undeniably brilliant pitcher — 30 or more wins three years in a row, nine other seasons with 20 or more wins, 80 career shutouts, and induction as one of the first five greats into the National Baseball Hall of Fame. By all accounts (or nearly all accounts), he was also a thoroughly admirable person. This facet of his character, Christy Mathewson as Frank Merriwell, is captured somewhat better in Eric Rolfe Greenberg's fictional "The Celebrant," I think, than it is in Robinson's biography.

Matty's early life gets only perfunctory treatment. Indeed, the author seems not to know for sure where Husk's hometown is. (The locals called him "Husk" in those days.)

Robinson writes: "To the north of Factoryville, in northeastern Pennsylvania, were the towering coal bunkers [breakers?] of Scranton, with Carbondale to the east." Wait a minute. Scranton isn't north of Factoryville, Matty's birthplace; it's southeast.

Nor does the book always get its quotations straight: The author writes of "Thayer's 'writhing pitcher grinding the ball into his hip.'" No. A direct quote can't be varied to fit the quoter's syntax. That "grinding" has to be "ground," as Thayer penned it. Near the end of the book Robinson suggests that Grantland Rice might have had Mathewson in mind when he wrote, "When the great scorer comes to mark against your name...." But that's not what Granny wrote. He wrote the properly metrical and slightly different, "When the One Great Scorer comes to write against your name...."

Okay, these are trivial matters, linguistic and geographical minutiae. But there are a few baseball matters as well. On page 49 Robinson puts Larry Doyle on the Giants' roster in 1904. Actually, he knows better, for later in the book he has Laughing Larry joining the team in 1907, when in fact he did. A few pages later Robinson credits Matty as "the second major league pitcher — Cy Young did it first for the Red Sox in 1901 — to win 30 or more games." That's true only if the history of the majors began in 1900, making it a blunder both unhistorical and noisy. (How great an achievement can it be if we're only talking about seven years worth of history?) Fella name of Radbourn won no fewer than 60 games for

Providence of the National League in 1884.

On page 59 Robinson relates an anecdote about the weak-hitting Cub outfielder Jimmy Slagle belting a home run off Matty in 1904. It's a charming story, but if SABRite Raymond Gonzalez, writing in the 1980 "Baseball Research Journal" is correct, and I believe he is, it never happened. The only Cub to hit a homer off Mathewson in 1904 was Frank Chance, on July 21st. On page 81 Robinson mentions (and lazily bobbles) "an eternal baseball trivia question: 'Which two pitching brothers won more games than any other brother combination?'" Scratch "eternal"; make it "ephemeral." The Niekro brothers and the Perry brothers have far outpaced Christy Mathewson and his winless sibling Henry.

There are a couple of other minor disappointments. The book lacks a table showing Matty's lifetime record in professional baseball. No doubt many readers will have access to The Baseball Encyclopedia, Total Baseball, Daguerreotypes, or some other source, but it still seems like an odd omission. Robinson's Gehrig biography lists the Iron Horse's complete stats.

Both biographies contain extensive acknowledgments, but neither has source notes. Yet there are direct quotes galore -- from where? One would expect a book from Oxford University Press to nail down its sources. If nothing else, checking them before publication would probably have eliminated some of the gaffes that slipped through.

Perhaps this review has been too harsh. "Matty: An American Hero" is not a bad biography. Many fans will enjoy the fine baseball writing, will learn a lot, most of it true, and won't give a hoot about the reservations I've expressed. It's just that Matty really was a sensational pitcher, even if he was less than the personal paragon portrayed by the "Gee whiz" journalists of his day, as Robinson calls them. (And maybe he was that paragon — my view is the Scottish verdict "not proved.") But on his baseball record alone, apart from his presumptive sanctity, a solid biography would be no more than Matty's due. This one is adequate, not definitive.

JERRY TOMLINSON is the author of "The Baseball Research Handbook."

Playing with the Big Ball

By T. Kent Morgan

THE KEY TO WRITING A book review is responsibility to both the writer and the reader. That's why it's important for me to tell you up front that two of my passions in life are books and softball. Therefore, when I read about "The Worth Book of Softball," I could hardly wait to get my hands on it.

I first came across a copy in St. Petersburg this March while on a spring training baseball and books pilgrimage. I kept flipping through it in bookstores and my initial reaction was disappointment. I was able to control my book-buying desire, and finally decided to wait until I returned to Canada to purchase it. After all, I already had five boxes of books to ship and another dozen or so books for my luggage.

When I arrived home, there was a postcard in the mail from the editor of this publication asking me to call him if I wanted to write a review. I did and the first book he suggested was this one. Was this fate? [Editor's note: Yes.]

In his introduction, Paul Dickson states this book is "intended as a valentine to a sport" played by over 40 million Americans and "it is hoped that you the readers see yourselves in this book because it was written for and about you the players." If that was the goal of Dickson, photographer Russell Mott and their editors, it can't be argued that they failed to accomplish it.

The text by Dickson, who is best known for his well-received baseball dictionary ("The SABR Review of Books," Vol. IV, 1989), celebrates the game as he promises.

THE WORTH BOOK OF SOFTBALL:
A Celebration of America's True National Pastime
By Paul Dickson
Photographs by Russell Mott
Facts On File, 1994, 276 pp., $22.95

Through a series of quotations in the introduction and a second chapter focusing on "The State of Game", it becomes clear why softball is a game for everyone.

As any softball bookaholic

> ## *The greatest female pitcher in history, [Joan] Joyce once faced Ted Williams. After 40 pitches, the 'Splendid Splinter' had managed one base hit and one foul ball.*

---

knows. little has been written about the history of the game. This is remedied in chapters 3 through 6 that take the game from the shores of Lake Michigan in 1887 to today's "sport of many games" as it has been described by Don Porter of the Amateur Softball Association (ASA). One version I didn't know about was Southern California's "Over The Line." I can hardly wait for summer to arrive so I can play

what Dickson calls a "hip, on-the-edge game" on the beaches of Lake Winnipeg.

Those four chapters are clearly the strength of the book. If the book covered nothing else, it would have been a valuable addition to softball literature. But Facts On File probably wouldn't have published it because most of those 40 million plus players are out playing the game, not lining up at bookstores wanting to read about its history.

In chapter 7, the author attempts to capture much of the essence of the game with "The Softballer's Miscellany." He calls it a collection of commandments, lists, rules, quotations and other softball mental equipment, including a thesis on naming teams. This sort of thing was done more successfully in other softball books such as "Dr. Whacko's Guide To Slow-Pitch Softball (Collier Books, 1991) and "The Irresistible American Softball Book (Doubleday Dolphin, 1978). An expansion of this miscellany would have added to the fun of the book and made it more attractive to the target market, the player.

As might be expected from Dickson, the book includes a glossary of softball terms. The value of this section is that it not only covers softball terms and slang but also clarifies differences in meaning between baseball and the many variations of softball. It is always

fun to learn new terms and my favorite is "airway" which the glossary calls "a term to describe the path that a ball goes through in underhand pitching." I can't wait to use it this summer with my Masters slow pitch team. Once the outfielders get back to position after chasing down another home run (here on the Canadian prairies we mostly play on open fields), I plan to turn around and loudly declare "that pitch must have been outside my planned airway."

While "The Worth Book of Softball" certainly will find a prominent place in my baseball/softball library (at minimum on a shelf, not on the floor), it is not without its deficiencies. Chapter 8 is an "Official Record Book" with a subhead proudly stating that "softball has never had a record book — now it does." I strongly disagree with that statement. The record book is compiled by Bill Plummer III, director of public relations and media, ASA and that is where the problem lies. The records cover 39 pages and almost all relate to Plummer's organization. How can this be considered a true record book when less than two pages are devoted to the United States Slo-Pitch Softball Association, an organization in existence since 1968 and boasting a 1992 membership of over 100,000 teams?

And I must take Dickson to task for his fiction bibliography. How could he possibly not include the best softball novel of them all, "Guys Like Us" by Tom Lorenz (The Viking Press, 1980)? This book on relationships both within a team and a marriage belongs right

> ## "No matter where they live or how well they play, most softball players agree on one point, winter is just too long. Play ball!"

at the top of any list of softball books.

The photographs by Russell Mott play a major role in this oversized book (8x10). He took over 10,000 photos during a two-year period in an "effort to capture the look and action" of the game. Unfortunately, too many of the photographs are static and fail to add anything. In many instances, photographs appear to be used strictly for graphic design purposes

with no relationship to the accompanying text.

In contrast, the historical photographs of the game, the majority provided by the ASA, are another strength of the book. However, I find it difficult to believe that any book that is described on the flyleaf as "a magnificiently illustrated tribute to the game of softball...and its superstars" doesn't include an individual photograph of Joan Joyce. Considered by most softball people to be the greatest female pitcher in history. Joyce once faced Ted Williams. After 40 pitches, the "Splendid Splinter" had managed one base hit and one foul ball.

While softball may be the game for everyone, I won't suggest this book is for everyone. However, if you are one of those people that Dickson describes so well in the following short paragraph, this book belongs on your bookshelf ready to be pulled down in January or February.

"No matter where they live or how well they play, most softball players agree on one point, winter is just too long. Play ball!"

T. KENT MORGAN is manager, public relations and communications, at Red River Community College in Winnipeg Canada. Player, coach, administrator, freelance writer and broadcaster, TV host, statistician, public address announcer, he has worn all those caps in a 30-year love affair with fast-pitch and slow-pitch softball. In 1993, he played for and coached his Masters team, the TKM Touring All-Stars, in the Slo-Pitch Canada 40-plus national championship, but says his real claim to fame is once getting a hit off softball's most famous pitcher, "The King," Eddie Feigner.

Love Is Not Enough

By Michael Gershman

THAT WILLIAM HARTEL loves Wrigley Field is immediately evident from his preface to "A Day at the Park: In Celebration of Wrigley Field." But Dr. Hartel, a dentist by trade, should by this time have acquired some aesthetic distance about his love object. Instead, his imitation of Rick Smolan's successful "A Day in the Life" series is wildly expensive ($29.95 for a mere 120 pages), indiscriminate in its praise of Wrigley, and badly in need of editing.

In the preface, Dr. Hartel says of Wrigley "The park has shrunken [!] as I have grown." On page 2, he notes that the Cubs were once known as the Orphans but doesn't explain why. The answer: their manager, Adrian "Cap" Anson, was also called "Pop"; when he was canned, they became "Orphans."

A DAY AT THE PARK:
In Celebration of Wrigley Field
By William Hartel
Sagamore, 1994, 120 pp., $29.95

On page 6, Dr. Hartel says that Charles Weeghman, owner of the Federal League Chicago Whales, leased the land at Clark and Addison on the understanding that "the cost of improvements could not exceed $70,000...Whether Weeghman secretly intended to violate the terms of his lease...we will never know." Yet, two pages earlier, the author uses a full page to show Weeghman's building permit with the cost of the building clearly listed at $250,000.

Thankfully, Dr. Hartel steps aside and gives writers (Roger Kahn), former Cubs (Hank Sauer), and umpires (Doug Harvey) a turn at bat. Although the vast bulk of the material is reprinted, there are notable excerpts from classic pieces like E.M. Swift's "One Place That Hasn't Seen the Light" and "Season Ticket" by Roger Angell.

As for the pictures, they range in quality from acceptable (grinning fans and arty shots of the ivy on the outfield wall) to utterly inexplicable (a full page color shot of peanuts opposite a full page color shot of popcorn).

All except the historical shots were taken on June 18, 1993 when the Cardinals met the Cubs in a Friday day game. There is no game story, just a box score. If I were to score this volume (I can't, in good conscience, call it a book), the line score would read no runs, three hits, four errors.

MICHAEL GERSHMAN is the author of "Diamonds: The Evolution of the Ballpark," winner of the 1993 Casey Award as best baseball book of the year.

Keeping the Players in Line

By David Nevard

"Never Just a Game" is an academic baseball book — it was written by a college professor and contains footnotes and an index. Some academic baseball books, even if they are biographies, are dry as dust. The subject here is baseball as a business, but Robert Burk has a good writing style which keeps the book moving along, despite massive quantities of facts and numbers.

The amateur ideal was short-lived in baseball. The New York Knickerbockers, an amateur social club recognized as the first modern baseball team, played their first game at Elysian Fields in 1845. Within fifteen years, "outside" players were being recruited by clubs and paid (under the table) for their services, while crowds of 1500 were paying 50 cents apiece to watch them play. Non-playing club members became entrepreneurs, and as Burk notes forlornly, "the former guardians of Yankee moral values and participatory traditions in baseball were finding their avenues of influence dwindling to being the self-appointed literary and journalistic consciences of the sport."

Professionalism led to touring clubs, and then to the first leagues — the National Association and its successor, the National League — and what the author calls the "bitter off-field struggles between players and management over prestige, power, and profits." Burk's stance is hardly neutral; in his view the owners' goal was "an all-encompassing system of labor serfdom."

Players' unions, strikes, lockouts,

NEVER JUST A GAME:
Players, Owners, &
American Baseball to 1920
By Robert F. Burk
University of North Carolina Press.
1994. Illustrated. 284 pp.
+ appendix (with charts),
notes, & index $34.95

salary-caps, revenue sharing, small markets vs. big markets: all these things were known to baseball fans of a century ago. While the reserve clause was the owners' main weapon, Robert Burk proposes a

---

Burk produces the most fascinating part of the book when he details the career of David Lewis Fultz, president of the ill-fated Players' Fraternity 1913-1917.

---

new theory: that rules-tinkering done in the early days (distance from mound to plate, number of balls per walk, etc.) was not just a process of refining the game, but was a method of controlling salaries.

Here's his logic: It's pretty well known that increasing offense tends to increase attendance. So the owners would naturally want to boost the scoring when they could. But, the author says, this also fattened batting averages, which raised

salary demands and the payroll. Since early teams carried few pitchers, most of the payroll went to the hitters. So when the owners wanted to contain salaries, they simply made offense more difficult by changing the rules.

Burk takes 44 pairs of batting average/salary years 1877- 1921. "In 31 of them, the direction of change of each statistic is the same: when offense goes up, salary follows [the year afterwards], and when batting averages decline, so do salaries."

31 out of 44 sounds convincing, but readers familiar with the work of Pete Palmer and Bill James are not going to be satisfied with a formula that equates batting average with offense. Salaries were not a matter of public record until fairly recently, and Burk's figures from a hundred years ago, derived from numerous sources, must contain a great deal of hearsay.

Burk cites two rule changes in 1888 — lowering the strikeout to three strikes, and no longer ranking walks as hits — and shows that batting averages declined by .035. His inference is that offense declined by that much, but of course only the first rule really affected offense. Walks = hits was only in effect for one season (1887), and it was probably just a silly idea that got laughed out of existence. Salaries went up a little after 1887, but they went up even more after 1888, despite plummeting batting aver-

ages! This was one of Burk's 13 deviant years; explained by the "trade war" with the American Association.

Mr. Burk admits that the owners left no paper trail of any plan to contain salaries by manipulating the rules. All the evidence is circumstantial, and Burk has a tendency to oversimplify in order to force his points: "In a desperate attempt to hold the line on future salary escalation...the National League adopted offense-suppressing rules changes. The owners approved a new five-sided home plate to improve umpires' vision of strikes and made a batter's first two foul balls strikes." The foul strikes are plausible, but the five-sided plate? Again, we learn of the 1904 rule that made 235 feet the minimum for fences. Scoring went down in subsequent seasons, but was there a direct connection? It would have been helpful to show if any teams actually had fences that short, and how their payrolls were affected by the new rule.

There is no listing of who was on the rules committees or where suggestions for rules changes came from, merely that they were approved by the owners. I believe the author overlooks the possibility that many baseball rules evolved along with the skill of the players — as pitchers became faster and more accurate, for instance, the tendency was to allow them fewer balls per walk and to move the mound farther from the plate.

There are also some factual errors. Ed Walsh is called a "slugger." Carl Mays is cited as one of the pitchers exempt from the 1920 anti-spitball rule; he was not. {The seventeen "grandfathered" spitballers, according to Martin Quigley in "The Crooked Pitch": Bill Doak, Phil Douglas, Dana Fillingim, Ray Fisher, Marvin Goodwin, Burleigh Grimes, Clarence Mitchell and Dick Rudolph in the NL; Doc Ayers, Ray Caldwell, Stan Coveleski, Red Faber; the original Dutch Leonard, John Picus Quinn, Allen Russell, Urban Shocker and Allen Sothoron in the AL.} Besides, consensus now is that it was probably a gray fastball that killed Ray Chapman, not a spitter.

Burk's strong point is industrial labor relations, and he produces the most fascinating part of the book when he details the career of David Lewis Fultz, president of the ill-fated Players' Fraternity 1913-1917. Fultz, a lawyer and former ballplayer, was hated by the owners and castigated in the press, but won some small victories for the players during the Federal League "trade war." When the FL folded and the MLB monopoly returned with salary-slashing vengeance, Fultz attempted to lead major and minor league players out

on strike for the 1917 season. Burk recounts in excruciating detail how the owners, alternating threats with appeals to self-interest, broke the union's solidarity.

"Ban Johnson exploited the breach between the union's leaders and its major league stars, claiming that Fultz's ultimate aims included the imposition of a wage scale and consequently the end of the star system...owners knew that the fraternity's major leaguer members were likely to be unwilling to strike, and therefore risk banishment, for minor leaguers threatening to take their jobs."

The players deserted the union, which folded the following year. Fultz, saying he'd had "the biggest disappointment of my life," went off to World War I as an aviator, returned to baseball as president of the International League (!), then quit the game, moved to Florida and set up a law practice. It would take another half-century for Marvin Miller to arrive on the scene and achieve David Fultz's dreams.

DAVID NEVARD lives in Waltham, Mass., and is the editor of "A Red Sox Journal." During the summer he can be found in Box 82, Row G, between third base and the left field wall.

The Next Step in the History

By Joseph Overfield

ALMOST FROM THE TIME minor league baseball began in the last century, its story and its statistics were faithfully recorded in The Sporting News, The Sporting Life (up to 1917), and in the annual guides, put out first by Spalding and Reach and later by TSN. There was a touch of minor league history in The Baseball Cyclopedia, written by Ernest Lanigan in 1922, and Baseball Magazine, from its inception in 1908, carried minor league articles. In 1944 Ralph Lin Weber published his pioneer (and still one of the best) team histories, "The Toledo Baseball Guide." In 1953, the National Association completed a 744-page monster, grandiloquently called "The Story of Minor League Baseball." It was neither a history nor an encyclopedia, but a mish-mash of facts and

---

THE ENCYCLOPEDIA OF MINOR LEAGUE BASEBALL
Edited by Lloyd Johnson and Miles Wolff
Baseball America, 1993, 416 pp. inc. bib., $34.95 paper; $42.95 hard cover

---

statistics, difficult to follow and certainly of little use as a reference work.

With the founding of SABR in 1971, opportunities for research and writing in the minor league field opened up, and such men as founder Bob Davids, Bob McConnell, Bob Hoie, Jerry Jackson, Ray Nemec, Art Schott, Joe Simenic, Dick Beverage, Bill Weiss, Cliff Kachline and the late Vern Luse applied their talents to the task. SABR's publication of "Minor League Stars I, II, and III" were several of the most valuable and successful projects undertaken by the organization. These books made recognizable to the average fan such minor league legends as Joe Hauser, Smead Jolley, Ike Boone, Jigger Statz, Buzz Arlett, Nick Cullop and Frank Shellenback.

After The Sporting News changed its format and practically abandoned minor league coverage, Baseball America, a biweekly publication, picked up the torch in admirable fashion. Over the last 30

years, scores of team and league histories have been written, plus a few overall minor league histories, all adding to the mix.

This mass of minor league material notwithstanding, W. Lloyd Johnson, historian, writer and former SABR president and executive director, felt there was still a niche unfilled. His plan envisioned an encyclopedia to contain a statistical story of each minor league season, compilations of all-time leaders for each league and for the whole spectrum of minor league ball, plus an almanac of all cities which had ever had minor league clubs. He quickly abandoned as unmanageable the idea of listing all the players. He submitted his proposal to several publishers but was rebuffed until he talked to Miles Wolff, publisher of "Baseball America," who not only agreed to undertake the project but also offered to assist with the compilations and the editing.

Johnson and Wolff, aided by a star-studded cadre of minor league researchers, mostly from SABR, have brought forth a marvelous book, logically arranged and crammed with so many facts and figures as to defy assimilation. It is a treasure trove for the browser, a gold mine for the researcher and a joy for the cover-to-cover reader (which I was) .

At the core of the book are the year-by-year standings for each league from 1902 to 1992. For the early years only the won-lost records, the games behind and the year's statistical leaders are given, but later on, names of managers, nicknames, attendance figures and even big league affiliations are included. All this is great, but the icing on the cake is the add-ons to each season, headed "This Date in Minor League History." One won-

ders, with so many facts provided, why it was not called "This Year in Minor League History." It is my understanding that most of this fascinating material was collected from an unpublished manuscript compiled over many years by SABR member Arnold Springer, a retired railroader from Estherville, Iowa.

Mention has been made of Hauser, Jolley and the boys. The Encyclopedia reminds us that there are many other career minor leaguers worth remembering. What of Jim Poole, who played professionally for 34 seasons — long enough for him to play in Florida East Coast League games with two of his sons! What of George Brunet, who played organized baseball for 32 consecutive seasons and struck out a record 3,175 in his minor league career? What of George Payne, who won 348 games in 26 years on the mound, and walked only 1.5 men for every nine innings he threw? What of Ray French, who played a record 2,738 games as a minor league shortstop in a career extending from 1914 through 1941? What of outfielder Raymond Perry, who hit 348 home runs, batted .323 over 18 seasons, led his minor league in homers seven years in a row, yet never played in a major league game? What of Clarence (Hooks) Iott, who fanned 25 batters in a nine-inning Northeast Arkansas League game on June 18, 1941, then less than a month later

whiffed 30 men in a 16-inning contest? And what of Ernest (Kid) Mohler, stalwartly built at 5-foot-4 and a half, carrying 145 pounds, who played a record 2,871 minor league games at second base — even though he was lefthanded?

Mind-boggling facts pop up everywhere. Take these three accounts of unassisted triple plays. June 19, 1911: In a game against Los Angeles, Walter Carlisle of Vernon (Pacific Coast League) turned an unassisted triple killing — from his position in centerfield. May 19, 1912: Roy Akin, third baseman for Waco (Texas League) snatched an attempted squeeze bunt and turned it into an unassisted triple play. The punch line: one year earlier Akin had *hit into* an unassisted triple play while playing for Los Angeles. The book doesn't say so, but I'm assuming Akin was the protagonist in both incidents. And how about an unassisted triple play being turned by a catcher? Happened in 1925 when Emmett Wiley of Cushing in the Southwestern League pulled the trick.

Strange things happen to leagues and individual clubs as well. In 1905, 21 different cities were represented in the Class C Ohio-Pennsylvania League, but only four completed the season. In 1985 the California League played the full season with nine teams. Did you know (I didn't) that Cleveland had teams in the Double-A American Association in 1914 and 1915? Or that, in 1905, the Kitty League had to suspend operations because of a yellow fever epidemic? Or that the Butte Copper Kings (Pioneer) had to suspend their August 22, 1922 game because of a snowstorm? And a final note to the attention of ex-National Football League Commissioner Pete Rozelle, who ordered his teams to play the weekend of the Kennedy assassination: on May 20, 1911, the Eastern League called off all its games because of the funeral of King Edward VII.

Accounts of tragedies of all kinds can be gleaned from the annual notes, none more shocking than the month of June 1951. On the 10th, Ottis Johnson of Dothan (Alabama-Florida) died after being beaned. On the 11th, a lightning bolt killed centerfielder Andy Strong of Crowley (Evangeline), and then on the 29th, 19- year-old Dick Conway of Twin Falls (Pio-

neer) died on the playing field after being struck in the heart by a thrown ball.

My great enthusiasm for this book and my awe at the magnitude of its research are diminished only slightly by some of its flaws. First of all, the book is truncated, in that it omits the first 25 years of minor league history. There are errors of fact and omission in the statistics. Examples: Alabama Pitts, famed jailbird ballplayer, made his debut with Albany of the International League, not the Georgia-Florida League. Alphonse (Tommy) Thomas was a righty, not a lefty. And Rick Lancelotti of Buffalo should be included (along with Ken Strong) as the all-time single season leader for the Eastern League. And one final cavil: the proofreading failed to pick up quite a few typos.

But overall, Johnson, Wolff and company have done a great job. No baseball library should be without The Encyclopedia of Minor League Baseball. Personally, I can't wait for the next edition.

Baseball historian JOE OVERFIELD is a regular contributor to this review and SABR publications.

Talkin' Baseball

By Larry Gerlach

A
S PIONEERED BY Lawrence Ritter's "The Glory of Their Times"(1966), "oral histories" — edited versions of interviews with former denizens of the diamond — have become a staple of baseball history and literature. Steven Banker, John Holway, Donald Honig, Walter Langford, and Eugene Murdock are among those who have made conspicuously important, even invaluable, contributions to the genre. Unfortunately, perhaps inevitably, the field increasingly has become glutted by volumes of superficial interviews that reveal little about the interviewees or the game. Oral history is easy to do, but difficult to do well.

Mike Blake, author of "The Minor Leagues: A Celebration of the Little Show," doesn't know

---

BASEBALL CHRONICLES:
An Oral History of Baseball
Through the Decades.
By Mike Blake. Betterway Books,
$16.95

---

quite how to describe "Baseball Chronicles." He characterizes it variously as the preservation of "first-hand recollections [that] would have been lost forever," as "a celebration of the game and those gentlemen (sic) who have made the game endure as a linchpin of Americana and the growing up of this great nation," and as an oral history of the game from "an unsophisticated and innocent age of baseball" when "the men who played the game were just there to play hard and have fun" to "the growth and sophistication of the current era." Notwithstanding such strained attempts to invest the book with greater importance than is warranted, Blake also forthrightly declares that his primary purpose was to write "just a fun-to-read slice-of-history book."

With contributions from 140

players ranging from Hall of Famers to one-game wonders and including a representative group of Negro leaguers, "Baseball Chronicles" is easily the most ambitious "interview book" published to date in terms of breadth and scope. It comprises nine chapters, one for each decade from the 1910s to the 1990s. Each chapter begins with a simplistic and idiosyncratic "overview" of the decade and a chronological listing entitled "selected decade highlights (in addition to those told in this chapter)." There follows what Blake calls "the good stuff" — i.e., player reminiscences arranged by the date of the episode recalled. Instead of autobiographical accounts or career remembrances, we have episodic stories about individual players and isolated performances.

The book begins with Chet Hoff recalling his strikeout of Ty Cobb on September 17, 1911, and ends with Dave Winfield reflecting on his shedding of the "Mr. May" label by doubling in the winning runs in the final game of the 1992 World Series. Each player's "chronicle" is preceded by a brief biographical sketch.

Such a wide-ranging collection of disparate stories requires an elaborate editorial apparatus to provide historical and interpretive context. Blake's attempt to provide back-ground and continuity for the "chronicles" is largely unsuccessful. His commentary is marred by a pretentious and awkward style, an unsure grasp of baseball history, an adulatory attitude toward ball players. The book's most serious weakness, however, relates to the stories themselves.

The basic problem is not that Blake sacrificed depth for breadth or that the stories vary greatly in quality. The fundamental problem is that there is no rationale for stories that are included other than that they were the stories the players happened to tell. For Blake the recording of the memories of ex-ball players is inherently important, whereas in truth few have anything important to say. The utterings of ballplayers per se are not significant and worth recording. Significance is determined by what is said, not the retelling itself.

Blake did not interview players, but simply asked them for a story, any story, to include in the book. He got what he asked for: any old story, interesting or insipid, dull or droll, from ballplayers whose sense of historical significance, capacity for recall, and ability to tell a story vary considerably. As Blake acknowledges: "Some guys just can't tell stories, or at least they can't remember any interesting ones." More to the point, Blake concedes: "These are not my favorite baseball stories; they are

the favorite tales of the gentlemen who lived them and chose to remember them here." We, too, wish that Mickey Mantle had talked about his 565-foot homer in Griffith Stadium in 1953, that Willie Mays had recalled his over-the-shoulder catch in the 1954 World Series, that Reggie Jackson had reflected on his three consecutive first-pitch homers in the 1977 World Series, and that Hank Aaron had commented on his record-setting 715th home run in 1974. Would that someone besides Larry Doby had discussed racial integration, and that anyone had addressed the strike of 1981. Blake didn't ask probing questions or elicit commentary about important episodes because "this is the ballplayers' book, not mine." More likely, he was less interested in collecting oral histories than obtaining "an entertaining nugget" or "a quick hit or two" from as many players as possible.

Curiously, Blake invoked an arbitrary "ground rule" that precluded the inclusion of seemingly relevant material. "Only baseball folk still alive at the time I was interviewing, who gave me stories expressly for this book, were included." Why? Are the interviews he conducted with Lyman Bostock, Lefty Gomez, Bruce Heinbechner, Roger Maris, Billy Martin, Thurman Munson, and Eddie Solomon prior to their deaths no less legitimate as "first-hand" stories? The flip retort — "my book, my rules" — is not an adequate explanation.

On balance, most of the stories are interesting and entertaining, but few offer anything new or important. We've heard most of the better tales before, albeit with varying degrees of detail or embellishment. There is no harm in repeating old chestnuts like Whitey Ford's rare relief appearance in a pennant-clinching game in Boston in 1955 and Bobby Bragan's tale of the "two envelopes" left for him by Birdie Tebbetts, his predecessor as manger of Milwaukee Braves. But there is harm in distorting history and perpetuating inaccuracies.

Blake understands that the passage of time can play tricks on the mind. Thus he carefully rechecked game accounts and statistics and unobtrusively provides parenthetical corrections and elaborations to the stories. He notes, for example, that Hoff fanned Cobb in his second, not first, major league appearance; that the Red Sox eventually beat the Yankees 10-5 on October 3, 1948; and that Don Newcombe had a league-leading 164 strikeouts in 1951. Still, misstatements and errors abound. It may not be terribly significant that Charlie Gehringer misunderstands the religious context of Hank Greenberg playing on Rosh Hashanah in 1934

and misplaces his game-winning homer in the 10th inning instead of the bottom of the ninth. But it is critical that Roy Campanella's story of his meeting with Branch Rickey in October 1945 is fundamentally at odds with the version contained in his autobiography "It's Good To Be Alive" (1959) and that Hank Aaron's comments about the Braves moving to Atlanta in 1966 and his hitting a homer in the 1972 All-Star game are contradicted by the accounts in his life story "I Had A Hammer" (1991).

In the end, this eclectic compilation is less than the sum of its parts. It is not an oral history so much as an anthology of individual anecdotes, a pastiche of memories derived from a bunch of major leaguers talkin' baseball. That can make for a delightfully good read — as long as you don't believe everything you hear.

LARRY GERLACH, professor of sport history at the University of Utah, spends more time researching baseball umpires than a supposedly sane person ought to admit.

The Centerfielder As Literary Phenomenon

By Ed Goldstein

'It may be noted here that the Yankees
are the least popular of all ballclubs,
because they win,
which leaves nothing to "if" about.'
— A.J. Liebling, 1962

LIEBLING, GREATEST OF BOXING WRITERS, DETESTED BASEBALL. The netherworld of the boxing gym, with its population of semi- to full-blown criminals and severely damaged perpetrators of the manly art appealed to his taste for the interestingly seedy. The sanitized environs of postwar baseball left his palate unsatisfied. Had he lived another 30 years the Met locker room would have made him feel right at home.

However astute his fistic observations, his assessment of Yankee baseball comes up short. While the Yankees as a whole left little to ponder in Liebling's time, on an individual basis there are as many ifs as any sports enterprise could conjure. The end of the Dynasty alone raises the questions: if Skowron's back had been healthy; if Kubek hadn't broken his neck in the Army; if Ford had pitched the opening game of the 1960 Series; the dozens of ifs that populate the seventh game of that memorable Series; and if Mickey Mantle...

Ah, Mickey Mantle. Glorious, foolish, exasperating Mickey Mantle. The Ultimate If. The physical embodiment of a team unlovable to all but its devotees, and an icon to those who Believe. The ifs surrounding Mantle, from his fragility, to the primitive nature of reconstructive surgery in the early '50s to his unwillingness to participate in the most rudimentary rehabilitation will keep Devotees debating and in sleepless agony for decades to come.

The number crunchers can tell you instantly that he is nowhere to be found on the all-time lists. Those who burn out at 33 do not attain 3,000 hits, or reach the levels of RBIs, runs and the rest that longevity brings. 500 home runs, yes, but not 600 or 700; the all time leader is a healthy and sober man named Aaron. Once third in lifetime homers, Mick is now eighth; and the worst stat of all: the final batting average of .298, withered away by the final years of propping up the carcass of the Dynasty. It is little consolation that Saint James (Bill to his friends) proclaimed Mantle the greatest player of the '50s in his "Historical Abstract." The immediate gratification of seeing him atop the lists is missing.

Recently, however, dollars have superseded the raw data in the encyclopedias. The insane world of the sports collectors has made Mantle the Golden God once more. His name, more than any other, is a magnet for the collector, and he has responded to that market by making himself more accessible to it, and his autograph in its millions of reproductions is the basic unit of exchange in the pack rat frenzy of the card show. He is, in his sixties, more popular than ever.

As befits a god, Mantle has been the subject of several books, dating from 1953 to the present. (Can you name *anyone else, in any field,* who had biographies written about him or her for *more than forty years while still alive?*) My own library contains at least 15 Mantle volumes, and I know of several I am missing. Beyond that are several more proudly showing a Mantle photo on the dust jacket, using his image as a surefire lure for snaring the book buyer. A typical example is "Five O'Clock Lightning," a disappointing book by Tommy Henrich. This book promised much from the Yankee outfielder known

for his intelligence and candor, but delivered instead the same old stories reground for contemporary consumption. Perhaps Henrich thought he was being public-spirited by recycling. In any event, his 260-page book contains two pages of relevant information about Mantle, addressing Henrich's role in converting Mantle from short-stop to outfielder in 1951. Nonetheless, there is Mantle on the cover, hinting to the devotee another fix of Mantle facts.

The amazing thing about the 41-year Mantle literary catalogue is how little it has changed over the years. Obviously, "The Mick" of the late 1980s contains more data than "The Mickey Mantle Story" of 1953. But stack them side by side, author by author —Epstein, Schaap, Hirschberg, Schoor, Shapiro and the ghost-assisted Mantle himself — it's all basically the same. You're guaranteed to find: the baby named for Mickey Cochrane; switch-hitting in early childhood by batting against left- and right-handed relatives; the career nearly ended before it began by osteomyelitis, the 19-year-old brought to the majors by a dazzled Casey Stengel... At this point you've either lost interest or you can recite the details yourself, depending on the depth of your devotion. Yet these books sell well: "The Mick" was a national bestseller for several weeks.

Trying to explain all this is as simple as biblical exegesis. If you are a Believer it isn't necessary to explain, and if you're not, volumes won't do the trick. Like the simplest of childhood stories that the kids want to hear over and over again, there must be a reason why the devotee can't stop. Mostly likely and most simply, I think the same processes carry Mick along as elected Ronald Reagan president. He means well, he makes us think nice thoughts as long as we don't think too long or too deeply and he is very happy to be whatever we want him to be, which is a symbol of what we remember as a happier, better time.

Which leads me belatedly and reluctantly to the subject of this essay, the latest volume of the Encyclopedia Mickeyanna, "Mickey Mantle, The American Dream Comes to Life." Described as a companion volume to the "videography" of the same name (that means

videotape to you and me) it is largely a collection of photos and skimpy text which once again tell The Story. [Sagamore, 180 pp., $24.95; special price available for those who purchase the book and videotape together.]

I was very unimpressed with the video, a bizarre amalgam of Mantle telling the old "Billy and me got drunk..." stories in his semi-dazed country-boy style, familiar '50s and '60s footage and a great deal of inappropriate Roy Orbison music in the background. I am much less impressed with the book. In its defense, I will note that the review copy I received did not have the photos in place, just large boxes with descriptions of what would go inside. However, so great is the sameness of the Mantle canon, that simply by reading each description, I knew immediately what the photo was. I've seen, and have in other books, all of the Mantle boyhood photos, Mantle testifying before the Kefauver Commission, the stadium shots with the arrows showing where the mammoth homers landed. The only people who would want this $24.95 book are precisely the people who have seen it all before.

But it will sell. It will sell for the same reason the Muslim faces east at the call to prayer, the Catholic fingers each bead in its turn as he recites the Rosary and the Jew does his recitation of the Torah each year. Repetition does not dull the faith of the truly faithful, it only reinforces it. Mantle transcends the Yankees, baseball, and ultimately himself. His omnipresence in the seminal Octobers of our generation and his perfect imperfections have burned his image into our consciousness. Admit it, even if you hate his guts, and the Yankees as well, the alliterative magic of his name cannot help but conjure an entire era in your mind.

Buy the book or ignore it, it is of little consequence. There will be another out this year, and doubtless more to follow. The Disciples are many, and lo, they all have typewriters. But what will follow will probably be tinged with sadness. The Betty Ford Clinic stay is recent history, and I write this within weeks of Billy Mantle's death in a rehab clinic, caused by the same devils of Hodgkin's disease and substance abuse that haunted Mickey himself. The last chapters promise to be grim.

But there will always be believers among generations born decades after his career ended. And they will wonder at his deeds and agonize at his failures. And when his father asks him who was the greatest player ever, a little boy just like the one named David Mickey Goldstein will answer, "Mickey Mantle."

ED GOLDSTEIN, after having embarked on a two-year adventure which left his career in transition, still happily has his family intact. He can be located in the near future somewhere between Chicago and North Carolina. Or maybe not.

The Art of the Broadside

By John Roca

A COUPLE OF DECADES into the future, in a dark abandoned warehouse somewhere in downtown Cleveland or Detroit, a group of silent determined baseball enthusiasts, skins pale from lack of sunlight, will be sitting in front of a battery of computer terminals, their faces all aglow in the blue-green light of numbers zapping across the screens. What they're doing is sending a Worm through the Internet, straight to the Cooperstown database.

Toward one end of the huge space of the warehouse, amidst the clickety-clack of the keyboards and the endless scroll of paper being spat out of the printers, a row of dusty wooden file cabinets stand, overflowing with sundry boxscores, newspaper clippings, graphs and charts. On the wall behind the cabinets, right behind the row of ashtrays growing gray tentacled colonies of cigarette butts, there will be a picture of Bill James.

After all, Bill James is the patron saint of a generation of number-crunching baseball cyberpunks. Most assuredly, James and his progeny share a number of attitudinal allegiances with the outlaw hacker generation: computers as a means to learn about the world, an insatiable hunger for information, a healthy mistrust of authority, and the promotion of decentralization, not to mention stuff like "fighting the power," "feeding the noise back into the system," and "surfing the edges." "Mondo 2000: A User's Guide to the New Edge" describes this modern age phenomena in detail.

In any event and regardless of one's views on cyberpunks, Bill

---

THE POLITICS OF GLORY:
How the Hall of Fame
Really Works
By Bill James
Macmillan, 1994, 384 pp., $23

James is known to the outside world primarily as a Sabermetrician. Nevertheless he rightly claims that he is primarily a statistician. However, it is James' writing ability that has established him as one of the premier baseball commentators of the last fifteen plus years. It is difficult today to appreciate the impact that his early "Abstract" series had on those of us who were insufficiently satisfied with The Sporting News Baseball Register. In this respect, we've become a bit spoiled with the proliferation of new and more accurate standards for measuring baseball performance. However, once Bill James introduced us to "batting runs," "similarity scores," "Brock6," and similar concepts, hardcore fans could no longer be content looking at the baseball world through the same small windows that were "batting average," "earned run average," and the like.

What was, and remains, most satisfying about James' writing was the fresh "badass" attitude that he carried. In this respect, a "badass" has been defined by Thomas Pynchon (no slouch in this category himself) as "bad meaning not morally evil...more like able to work mischief on a large scale. What is important here is the amplifying of scale, the multiplication of effect." Clearly, James' mission in life is to likewise work "mischief" on the Game through his inexhaustible search for Truth with a capital T. Undoubtedly, James' work has had an enormous impact on how baseball is written...and understood.

As Merritt Clifton, another baseball "badass," once said in refer-

> **His rant on this issue shows that he hasn't lost his delightfully crotchety touch.**

ence to the Hall of Fame, "perhaps sedition spreads." He could have been writing about Bill James.

"The Politics of Glory" is James' latest broadside, devoted this time around to the Hall of Fame. Here he expands upon themes which he first touched upon in the first section of "The 1988 Baseball Abstract." In this regard, "The Politics of Glory" is James' most substantial writing exercise since his seminal "Historical Baseball Abstract." To the extent that he elaborates on the polemic issues regarding the Hall of Fame to which he referred earlier, "The Politics of Glory" must be considered an important book.

Here James presents the Hall for what it is: an institution which originated as an idea for community development in the economically depressed village of Cooperstown, New York, yet has become a some-times distant monolith that has never fully confronted its mission. James passionately describes the Hall's fundamental failure: to deter-mine how many players deserve to be honored with induction, and then, how these players are to be identified. But because the Hall has never addressed these institutional issues head-on, James indicts it for taking halfway measures and avoid-ing its responsibility.

James' compelling history of the Hall reveals the many institutional problems inherent in the selection procedure which aggravate the Hall's structural deficiencies. Thus, James' thorough analysis demon-strates that the flawed voting process entrusted to the Baseball Writers' Association of America (BBWAA) results in failure to achieve consensus, which was par-ticularly frustrating in the early years. Likewise, early selections by the Veterans' Committee destroyed any notion that the Hall should be the exclusive province of only the greatest players, thereby making it even more difficult, if not impossi-ble, to ever achieve a general con-sensus regarding those players who should be inducted. James points out that this lack of objective stan-dards makes it difficult (if again,

not impossible, given the amount of time which has passed since the first inductions,) to adopt more stringent standards of admission. New standards tightening the admission process will certainly be perceived as unfair.

This lack of foundation to sup-port the Hall's election standards, which have led to the induction of marginal candidates, is what is especially frustrating to James, who has always taken pride in support-ing his arguments with solid research. It is not unexpected that James would attribute the cacopho-ny of uninformed voices seeking the induction of a myriad of players, from Rocky Colavito to George Cutshaw, to the inherent deficien-cies in the Hall. The rhetoric and bias become deafening in this mael-strom of misguided opinion. Even a cursory review of a chapter which James dedicates to a collection of quotes taken from letters to the edi-tors of well-known baseball publica-tions provides more than a vivid illustration of the forces that are at work in this contested arena.

To more fully illustrate this effect, James selects Phil Rizzuto, the subject of a well-orchestrated campaign initiated by the New York media, as a central figure in "The Politics of Glory." James does this not to malign Rizzuto, or even necessarily to campaign against the shortstop. Instead Rizzuto becomes James' subject for demonstrating

the appropriate care and analysis which should go into nominations to the Hall of Fame, which unfortunately is more often the subject of emotion instead. In the end, Rizzuto appears to be more the victim of the downpour of rhetoric than someone who has been somehow maligned by any failure to be inducted.

Rizzuto is also used to illustrate trends in the voting process. For example, James uses the Rizzuto case to show why some players decline in the balloting over time. James' research indicates that this is a function of two factors: 1) the appearance of another competitive player with greater credentials and 2) the change over time in the perception of the value of statistics. Similarly, James uses Don Drysdale to demonstrate the effect peak performance has on a player's opportunity for selection, as opposed to career-long consistency. These and other masterful examples illustrate the unspoken biases which operate on Hall of Fame voters.

James does not limit himself to the subtle trends evident in the Hall's selection procedure. He also unflinchingly describes the sometimes not-too-subtle politics prevalent in the Hall's administration, as well as the influence, or lack thereof, of persons in positions of responsibility regarding the Hall. James'

research efforts are quite evident in these sometimes gossipy sections. Although it is not clear what the drinking habits of Lee Allen and Ernie Lanigan, as well as those of sportswriters in general, have to do with anything else, James' display of institutional history is quite informative, as well as funny. "The Politics of Glory" was clearly not intended to lavish undeserved praise on those who compose the Hall of Fame.

As a publicly-funded institution, the Hall of Fame should be subject to rigorous scrutiny: not only its finances and inadequate processes, but also its personnel. After all, the Hall holds its collection in trust. As a result, it must be held to the same standards to which other publicly-funded institutions are subject.

Besides, public institutions can always use a good kick in the ass.

Thus, James proposes that the voting structure be turned over to five voting blocs: the fans, the media, the players, baseball professionals, and a so-called "scholars" group. Quite reasonably, James believes that these groups, through a revamped voting procedure, would eliminate fluke nominations, reasonably restrict the number of inductees and otherwise increase interest in the Hall itself.

The proposed format is indeed thought provoking. For one thing, while he has never been accused of

being a populist, James' suggestions concerning the "scholars" group smacks of snobbish elitism. He proposes high fee requirements, test-taking and notions of exclusivi-

> *James tackles not only the explainable phenomena of the Game, such as who was better, Joe Gordon or Rizzuto, but also weightier subjects such as the effects of destiny on greatness.*

ty, to keep out "the people who want to take the test so they can sit on bar stools and brag about how well they did." One is hard pressed to find fault with bragging, or with bar stools, or with bars, for that matter.

If James fails in any portion of "The Politics of Glory," it is in the scattered chapters where he details his statistical methods and how they tend to indicate which players should or should not be in the Hall. In this regard, James' "similarity score" technique is especially appropriate for discussing potential Hall of Fame candidates. However, the fault is not found in the concepts which James uses. He has always proven himself adept at setting forth adequate explanation for his methodology. Neither is the fault to be found in the conclusions he reaches. Rather, the problem is that these chapters become at times tiresome and frustrating to the reader, especially when they appear to consist of the rehashing of arguments James has made in the past. It is not that James has expressly made the same contentions in previous publications, but that they do not appear to necessarily lay any new statistical ground. Further, these chapters are sometimes frustrating in the way that they break the careful chronological narrative of the Hall's history which James has constructed.

Nonetheless, James is well aware that statistics are not the end-all. He recognizes the value of anecdotal evidence, and other subjective standards which should be taken into consideration when evaluating a player's standing on the pathway to Glory. Indeed, James makes it a point to note during several passages that he is a centrist — neither committed to the "right wing," which advocates total reliance on

the numbers, nor to the "left wing," which wants to do away with statistical underpinnings. As James notes, "There is some truth in what everybody is saying, and there's a lot of bullshit on both sides."

Of course, Bill James is not infallible. As a result, notwithstanding his never ending efforts to be objective and support his contentions with the results of his research, even he at times takes positions which seem biased. In a splendid chapter comparing the careers of Joe Tinker, who is in the Hall, and George Davis, who is not, James' analysis of the historical record abundantly demonstrates that George Davis is undoubtedly the best player not in the Hall. However, he questions whether or not anything would be gained at this time by inducting him. "George Davis is dead. He is forgotten. I can't see that it would accomplish a hell of a lot to vote him a plaque now."

James does not appear to make a hell of a lot of sense with this stand. James himself recognizes that Davis was "lost to history" by 1920, a good sixteen years before the first Hall inductees. If Davis was forgotten by 1936, does this mean he should not be inducted simply because of the voters' lack of long-term memory? Of course not. While one could personally not care one bit whether or nor George

Davis is inducted into the Hall, James' position is inconsistent with his desire that the Hall be the resting place of the Game's great players.

James can also engage in rhetorical games when he wants to, and when it comes to Pete Rose, he does. In the past, James has done a convincing job of showing that Rose was railroaded by Bart Giamatti. Whether or not one agrees with James' view of the evidence in this regard, James cannot be faulted for presenting his views objectively. Nevertheless, James makes a compelling case that notwithstanding Rose's unjust banishment from baseball, he should still be denied induction because of his present status.

However, after rationally discussing those burning Rose issues, James throws himself into an emotional tirade concerning whether or not Pete Rose would have prevailed in court battles with baseball. Clearly, this is a subject James knows nothing about.

It's stuff like this that can get you riled at Bill James. On the other hand, his rant on this issue shows that he hasn't lost his delightfully crotchety touch.

However, any negative aspects of "The Politics of Glory" are negligible when the book is judged in its

entirety. Bill James' writing is as powerful as ever, and the outstanding narrative and anecdotal data make this his best effort yet. While one cannot denigrate his earlier work (his Abstract series reads as fresh today as it did during the late '70s and early '80s), "The Politics of Glory" indicates that James is at his best when he focuses on one discrete topic.

"The Politics of Glory" will be an important book not solely because of its description of the Hall, but because, as James has always done, it teaches us more about baseball. James here tackles not only the explainable phenomena of the Game, such as who was better, Joe Gordon or Rizzuto, but also weightier subjects such as the effects of destiny on greatness.

In a wonderful chapter, which should have served as the book's conclusion, James expounds at length about the parallel universes of Rizzuto and Jerry Priddy. Therein, he exposes the degree of cosmic fate which influences and ultimately permeates the question of greatness. How Priddy could somehow get himself on some collective unconscious shit list, while Rizzuto, with a similar beginning, becomes the focus of concerted efforts to obtain his induction is ultimately unanswerable. Even for Bill James.

But who knows. Maybe James has really touched upon something here. Perhaps James' story about the diverging paths of two players to and from the beacon of Glory leads to notions that had never really been considered before. It could someday happen that those cyberpunks hacking away at keyboards in the bowels of an abandoned old building in the midst of an urban industrial wasteland will develop formulas to quantify all that stuff.

If fate and destiny and all that jazz can be quantified, who knows, even Herb Score could laugh at the unknown and make the Hall of Fame.

JOHN ROCA writes and publishes "TTT - Tribe Tract and Testimonial," a regular newsletter about the Game and its Cleveland connections.

Holding on to the Past

By Bob Bailey

EMORY IS A FUNNY thing. Without fairly constant reinforce-ment humans tend to forget things over time. Even with prodding there are some things that just don't stick where they should (my wife's birthday and our anniversary being two exam-ples).

Occasionally these memory lapses are self-inflicted. Mountains of articles and books have stated that Jackie Robinson was the first black to break the color line in the major leagues. Somehow Fleet Walker's 1884 sea-son with Toledo of the American Association is forgotten. Who won the first World Series? Most would answer, "Boston, 1903," when the real first World Series took place the same year as Walker's debut, when the National League Provi-dence Grays swept the American

Association New York Mets.

Baseball has done itself a good bit of harm by artificially bifurcat-ing its history between the 19th and 20th centuries. The game underwent no massive change in the way it was played over the win-ter of 1899-1900. If you really want to identify a mod-ern era, here are two that make more sense than the 1900 break: 1893, when the pitching distance was moved to the present sixty-feet-six, or 1920 when the Ruthians washed away the "Dead Ball" Era.

Baseball was played and records were set before the close of the Spanish-American War. One of the locations that is rich with the histo-ry of the game but has been obscured by time and a quirk of political fate is Louisville, Ken-tucky. A charter member of the

---

LEGENDS OF LOUISVILLE
Major League Baseball in Louisville,
1876-1899
By Philip Von Borries
Altwerger & Mandel, 1993, 153 pp. +
Index and Appendix, $24.95

National League, the events associated with this forgotten franchise include: the first NL shutout, the first major league gambling scandal, the Louisville Slugger bat, the first appearance of a black in major league contest, the first ballplayers' strike, and the first worst-to-first turnaround in baseball history. But more than events, it was the players who romped and swaggered across the Louisville diamonds that gave the city its baseball heritage.

In "Legends of Louisville," Philip Von Borries attempts to reawaken these memories and shake the dust off this legacy. Von Borries, a contributor to many articles on the 19th century game, and the winner of the Eclipse Award for his turf reporting (the award and a 19th century ballpark were named for the same horse), has produced a very different type of book. It makes no pretense to be a definitive franchise history, although the introduction and prefatory material in each section provide a solid overview of the development of the club. The "Legends" in the title are a combination of player profiles and player and team pictorials.

Thirty-four players are given a place in the book: from the ill-fated Jim Devlin on the 1876-77 NL squad to pitcher Gus Weyhing, who toiled briefly for his hometown team in the mid-1890s. In between we meet Guy Hecker, who had several extraordinary seasons as a pitcher (52 victories in 1884) and batter (hitting .342 in 1886 along with 26 pitching wins); William Van Winkle Wolf, blessed with the all-time moniker "Chicken"; Fred Clarke, who became a Hall of Fame player and manager after getting off to the fastest start of any rookie ever — five for five in his first game; and a barrel-chested rookie from the Paterson (N.J.) club who developed into the game's greatest shortstop, Honus Wagner.

Louisville was never much of a team. They had several seasons in their tour of the Association where they were in pennant contention into September; in 1890 they actually won the pennant. But usually they were either middle-of-the-pack, or just plain awful (particularly in 1889 and during their NL tenure of the 1890s). Their fate was financially driven: always short of operating cash, they relied on young, inexpensive talent to stock the club. And what talent it was. Players who made their major league debuts with Louisville include: Pete Browning, Tom Ramsay, Icebox Chamberlain, Lave Cross, John Ewing, Scott Stratton, Nick Altrock, Topsy Hartsel, Hughie Jennings, Deacon Phillippe, Rude Waddell and Dan McGann as well as the aforementioned Devlin, Hecker, Wolf, Clarke and Wagner.

But Von Borries' favorite is

clearly Pete Browning. The Browning chapter is the longest and most detailed, filled with Browning as a player and a man. It is not always a pretty picture. Browning was an inveterate drinker and in no small measure a buffoonish character. Von Borries claims that a physical infirmity, mastoiditis, was a mitigating factor in Browning's behavior. But for all his faults and lapses, Browning could hit. Three batting titles and a .341 lifetime average attest to his prowess as a batsman. And Browning also demonstrated a consistency found only among the greatest of players: for the ten years from 1882 through 1891 he finished lower than third in the batting race only once.

The narrative is only part of this book. The illustrations are fully a third of the volume. All but two players are shown in single shots. These include familiar studio shots of Browning, Hecker, Dummy Hoy and Fleet Walker. But there are also photos of Tony Mullane sporting his handlebar mustache and a young Honus Wagner early in his Pittsburgh career. There are also eight team photos among the 49 illustrations. In addition to a shot of an early 1870s amateur team, the Eagles, perhaps the most interesting team photo is of the 1877 Louisville Eclipse. This was an amateur-semi-pro squad that would evolve by 1882 into Louisville's entry in the Association. Seated in the middle of the first row is a somber, 16-year-old Pete Browning (were his ears bothering him already?).

The book closes with an assemblage of miscellany including all-time and season rosters, 1890 World Series line scores and data on managers and club presidents.

"Legends of Louisville" presents a roster of good and great players who graced the Louisville squad during their major league sojourn from 1879 through 1899. The profiles from the Association period are quite good and provide an interesting insight into the achievements of those players. The profiles of the players from the 1890s NL period look at many big names that passed through the Bluegrass City, Several are so short (just a few paragraphs) that they offer just a cursory look at the player.

But overall "Legends of Louisville" adds to the literature a narrative and pictorial review of one of the last century's forgotten franchises.

BOB BAILEY, author of several articles about Louisville baseball history, has in his garage (for reasons his wife cannot comprehend) the original tombstone of Pete Browning.

Interview:
Ken Burns

By Dick Johnson

ONLY FORTY YEARS OLD, KEN BURNS has already created a lifetime's worth of film production and won enough awards to fill a small museum. He stands as the filmmaker who has uniquely limned the essence of American civilization through his many documentaries. His subjects have ranged from the Brooklyn Bridge to Kingfisher Huey Long and his masterpiece, "The Civil War." Each has combined thorough and flawless research with artful narration and superb use of primary source material. Burns has set the standard for documentary film, and already has projects on his drawing board stretching into the next century.

It is the good fortune of baseball lovers and historians that Burns turned his attention to baseball. Starting more than four years ago Burns began work on what was planned as a ten-hour film of the Game and now has nearly doubled in length. Sponsored by General Motors and narrated by former NBC news anchor John Chancellor, "Baseball" promises to document the history of the game while revealing its heart and soul as well. The series will air in mid-September on PBS stations across America, nearly twenty hours of air time, divided into nine segments called innings.

I recently spoke to Ken Burns as he took a break from working on the final edit of "Baseball."

DJ: This is really a dream project I'm sure. Was it one that you had wanted to do or was it one that you were approached with?

KB: All of my projects are self-initiated, within limits. I was sitting in a bar in Washington, D.C. with my long-time collaborator, Mike Hill, at the very beginning of our project on the history of the Civil War. He suggested that baseball might be an apt subject after the Civil War was done, and the idea hit me like a lightning bolt. I realized with a certainty that I felt in very few projects that this was absolutely true, and we went on, finished "The Civil War" and began "Baseball." And as the last four years have borne out in nearly every day, this is really the true sequel to the earlier project. "The Civil War" is, as many people have called that horrible four years, the American "Iliad."

"Baseball" is an opportunity to look at the country that the Civil War made. And because of its wonderful object of "coming home," it's very much like an odyssey. So I think we're suggesting that in a Homeric sense the epic story of baseball might be our American "Odyssey."

It touches on themes so important to us, first on a broad sociological level — pain, race, labor and management struggles, integration and assimilation, the role of women, the nature of heroes, popular culture and advertising — all of those things are there. Then below that in a much more personal vein this game of ours — unlike any other constant in our national narrative — touches very powerful themes of time, family, memory and home.

DJ: Were there any authors or books that particularly inspired you as you were doing the background work on the project? Certainly those of us who were absorbed by the Civil War film you did were struck by the feeling Shelby Foote brought to the program as well in expertise but a real sort of heartfelt, well, how shall I say this? — you almost thought he was there. Was there anyone in your experience working on the baseball project that brought that to you?

KB: There are many people. I think in terms of counting influences I would have to say four writers really had a profound effect on how I began to approach the project, and then through their gra-

ciousness in appearing on camera helped us really understand the sport. They are Roger Angell, whom I think everyone agrees is the best baseball writer ever; Robert Creamer, who used to write for Sports Illustrated, and has written eloquently on Babe Ruth and the summer of '41 and other baseball subjects; Dan Okrent, who edits the tremendously popular "Ultimate Baseball Book" and several others, appears on camera more than anyone else in our film; and the poet Donald Hall, whose soaring metaphors about baseball really touched a place in my heart, is also quite moving and eloquent on film. He said at one point toward the very end, "This [meaning baseball] is the place where memory gathers."

That struck me as what this whole film was about. As we look at our national narrative, as we see how tired and overused our political narrative of wars and presidents and generals has become, particularly in an age of media cynicism, where we have almost destroyed the thing before it's born, we see that there are very few things that are constant, and one thing is baseball.

DJ: What were some of the moments in the film that made you laugh, and what were some of the ones that might have made you even start to cry?

KB: Well, it's funny that you said that. I thought that when I began to advertise this film to myself and then to others, as I began work on it I said that here I was very fortunate, that my men were all playing in fields rather than dying in them, as the Civil War's five years of efforts had produced a great tragedy, and I looked forward to the great humor of baseball, the anecdotes, the language, the colorful characters. And they are there aplenty in this series. But I realized very early on in the editing that I was really making a sequel to "The Civil War"; not that it's a downer, not that it's tragic, but that particularly because the central underlying theme of our series is about race, and it forms an incredibly potent follow-up to the themes of the Civil War. Our tension as a republic it seems to me is primarily about race. We formed the most glorious union but counted a black as 3/5ths of a person and fourscore and five years later we began a war which settled the question in a statutory fashion but certainly did

not solve it in the hearts and minds of men and women in our country. It's interesting to note that the next real significant progress in civil rights (after the Civil War) occurred not in the back of a bus, not in a lunch counter, not in a school, not in the armed forces, but on the baseball fields. And it makes Jackie Robinson's arrival on April 15th, 1947 not just an important wonderful glorious date in the history of our national pastime, but indeed in our republic. I would say further that in the remarkable example of Jackie Robinson, we see a heroic figure for all people for all time. It's one of the great stories in the human drama.

DJ: I see where you devote a portion of one of the innings to the Red Sox.

KB: Well actually in "The Civil War" we chose to focus on one particular Northern soldier and one particular Southern soldier, and periodically focused on one particular Northern town and one particular Southern town. We knew it's impossible for film to be encyclopedic. So it's important to find in our individual grains of sand a universe of common experience. And we've done that again in the baseball series. We've chosen not to focus on, but to return to the Red Sox and to return to the Brooklyn Dodgers and later the L.A. Dodgers, as a way of following some threads across the whole history of the game.

Baseball begins in New York City in the 1840s and Brooklyn teams are involved. Brooklyn is a National League team; it's got a wonderful checkered history, filled with more losses than wins, which is of course true of the game of baseball and the game of life. It witnesses in my opinion the finest moment in the history of baseball, when Jackie Robinson begins to play. It has finally a glorious victory over the Yankees in the 1955 series and then two years later the ultimate tragedy of being wrenched from its community and really destroying the fiber of that community. It has its share of glorious individuals from Sandy Koufax to Charles Ebbets himself, the man who built the ballpark and owned the team.

In the American League we have the last team to integrate, the Red Sox. As one of the early powerhouses in major league baseball,

they won a huge number of World Series, plus had this wonderful sort of myth of failure attached to them from selling Babe Ruth, and classic characters in Williams and Yastrzemski and Fisk and others. Plus, they're my team.

DJ: Do you think that the tragedy of the Red Sox, the defining moment of the persona of the team, might not have been the selling of Ruth and the other stars to the Yankees in the early '20s, but may well have been that afternoon in 1945 when Jackie Robinson was given what was called at the time a perfunctory tryout with the Red Sox? Here was the town that had really been a hotbed of abolition during the Civil War, of tolerance, education, and ironically a town that had seen athletes integrate other professional sports, namely hockey and basketball.

KB: Well we absolutely mention that moment in '45. I think when you really scrutinize it, it's more symbolic in retrospect than it was at the moment. I don't think baseball in '45, believe it or not, was ready. Rickey was plotting amongst his cohorts but it was by no means public. And it isn't until the end of the year in October that he scouted Robinson and said he was going to hire him for the Royals. No, I would have found it in the myth of Babe Ruth, but I don't want to subscribe to that entirely. I want to be able to look at the Red Sox and say, "My goodness, this is a game in which we celebrate losing." In football and in basketball when the chips are down, you just generally go to your quarterback who's going to complete 70% of his passes, or your guard who's going to hit 70% of his baskets, a Joe Montana, a Michael Jordan. But in baseball your greatest star can bat only one-ninth of the time. And if he fails only seven times out of ten he will end up in the Hall of Fame.

It's in the context of the way baseball reminds us of this almost inevitable expectation of loss that we find the source of the Red Sox great tragedy as well as the Yankees great triumph over the years for example. I mean you can't do a history of baseball without spending a lot of time with the New York Yankees.

DJ: I found that the thread that sort of tied "The Civil War"

together and in fact really quite a bit of the work that you do is the music. I've always found the choices very apt and flowing right with everything. How did you choose the music for "Baseball" and what were some of the themes that you chose to pursue? Did you have this scored independently or did you go back to some of the traditional music that has been associated with the game over the years?

KB: Well, I never score a film. Scoring is to me a rather cold and clinical application of music after the editing is done. In fact we recorded our music — most of it that's original to this production — before we began editing. This film is filled with literally dozens of renditions of "Take Me Out to the Ball Game." Some you will not believe. It's a beautiful song, incredibly malleable, and we think very poignant. We also have several versions of the "Star Spangled Banner." We also went into the archives of the Hall of Fame and various other archives and chose many other baseball tunes and arranged them and rearranged them and played them so "Hurrah for the National League Game," "The American League Two-Step," and "The Champs of 1912," among many others, form themes that run throughout the entire history.

At the same time the film covers more than 150 years of baseball and American history, and so we're accompanying it with the popular music of the time. So we have Basie and Ellington and Lester Young and Elvis Presley and R&B and Otis Redding and Iron Butterfly and Red Hot Chili Peppers and ragtime piano rolls. We have versions of tunes ala Stefan Grappelli and minuets and sort of 19th parlor music all the way through.

I really believe this soundtrack is the richest I've ever done and will probably be the sort of a history of American music at the same time it's a history of baseball, and we believe the history of the country.

DJ: That's wonderful fun. What were some of the more dramatic things you were able to uncover in terms of film footage of the game. The earliest film I'm aware of is what Edison shot back about 1899. Were you able to find things from that era?

KB: Yes, we have some stuff from the first decade that's pretty nice, including the 1909 World Series, and the New York Giants of 1904-1905. There's nothing that we can really use to edit a scene together but certainly we're no strangers to making things come alive with still photographs. In fact I had some footage of the 1908 season at the Polo Grounds and I chose not to use it in favor of telling the complete story of the Merkel boner (in more than 20 minutes) with still photographs. Because I felt that having a moving picture which was stuck in there was gratuitous. And the way we were treating these old photographs of the scene, we could make it move in a different way, we could bring some emotional sort of movement to the way we told the story.

DJ: Who would you say was probably the oldest and the most experienced of the witnesses to the game? I'm thinking that there may have been a photographer or someone who worked in a press box as a boy that went back to say the 'teens. Was there anyone of that era?

KB: We have what I think is an incredibly wonderful interview with Shirley Povich, the great Washington Post sportswriter, who has been covering baseball for more than half a century at the Post. He could remember vividly Walter Johnson's triumph in the 1924 World Series. Dating back even earlier we interviewed a 100-year old Yankee named Chet Hoff who remembers striking out Ty Cobb. There are many people like that but beyond a shadow of a doubt I believe the interview that people will most remember (if this series has a Shelby Foote) is a man named Buck O'Neill, a former Kansas City Monarch, and one of the most remarkable human beings I've ever met. I say that uncategorically. He just makes you feel better about being alive. He has a deep understanding of the game and he is remarkable in the way he brings the old Negro League life to life for us. And he is very gracious in understanding these very complex and, for many people, bitter themes. I believe he is going to be a wonderful healing force for the country.

DJ: Was there a single image in the film that inspired you more

than any other, one where you might want to stop the projector and run it back again, one particularly inspiring segment of the film?

KB: For the most part it's all a glorious tapestry. But as you asked the question I instantly thought of on an image of the Hanover, New Hampshire, town green in the mid-1880s. Just off to the side is Dartmouth College, where the common is criss-crossed not with sidewalks but pathways. Cut out among this strange geometry and weird composition of the directions of the paths is a baseball diamond. There is a fence and some kids and some adults are watching a baseball game in progress. Lining the exterior of the frame are the houses along the side of the green that begin to head down to the main street business district. I realized there was a moment and there were many moments in the history of the country when this game was a complete mirror of who we were. But there's the other side. We're dealing with a series that is 20 hours long and that includes a good deal of time on a gambling scandal that banned the game's favorite players for life in the 19th century; there are owners who fire their managers every year and are despised by their fans in the 19th century. You meet men whose careers are ended and cut short by their addiction to drugs in the 19th century. You meet people who complain that baseball isn't what it used to be back in the 1850s, when they were a boy. There's a sense of this constancy to the game, and the sense that it is a mirror of any particular era that you're in, so that when the labor agitations at the end of the 19th century began to really blossom, John Montgomery Ward of the New York Giants founded his ill-fated Players League, "the Brotherhood," and formed a new league. You've got wonderful correspondences, you know when Mike Milliken goes to jail, so does Pete Rose.

You begin to see the game as a precise mirror of where we are in the country and at the same time this one thing that seems a constant not of this time. As Donald Hall said that you could look at baseball and say that the daily life of America was the opposite of this, and that I think is an incredible statement.

DJ: During your research on this series, did you view some of the recent documentaries? Some of them I would rank with the best ever

— namely Irv Drasnin's "Forever Baseball" which was on the "American Experience" series, and the two HBO documentaries which made use of home movie footage shot by players and fans.

KB: I think that they are both totally different from what I've done; I've seen parts of all that you described except for the second version of the HBO special. I find the HBO stuff wonderful to look at but not really films. They're kind of nostalgic evocations of baseball, and nostalgia really ultimately does a disservice because it doesn't present any warts. Irv's piece lasts an hour and it's almost impossible to do anything but sort of kiss the subject, and that's what he did. What we're attempting is a really broad narrative of baseball in the same spirit of "The Civil War." You'll recognize the structure and the pacing is stylistically consistent with my work.

DJ: Now that you're in the home stretch, is there anything that you would have changed about this, would you have maybe added an extra inning or two?

KB: No, we started off and thought that this would be nine one-hour segments. It's now nearly 20 hours, and though I have my regrets that there are many wonderful scenes that I wish could be in this but just for the dynamics of editing can't be. We had a marvelous scene on Casey Stengel's testimony before the Kefauver Commission, which is riotously funny. There was a section on superstitions in baseball, and many, many scenes that had to go just because the Aristotelian poetic demanded that they be cut out of the film. You remember the great scene in "Amadeus" where Mozart is criticized for having "too many notes"? The notes might be beautiful but there are too many.

The process itself is organic; it's something we feel, it's something that we approach and we struggle with. We don't know in advance what we'll do. We put our arm around the game and try to take back as much of its glory and its warts as possible, and in doing so present a portrait of it which we think speaks to this larger sense that I have about what it is to be an American, about what it is to participate in something. Arthur Schlesinger says that there is too much pluribus

and not enough unum today, and I think if I had to describe what my own work is about thematically is sort pointing towards unum. Abraham Lincoln said the mystic chords of memory will one day call to the floor what he said were the better angels of our nature. I think that trying to find the better angels of our nature in this dark and funny, complicated story of baseball has been my mission for the last four years.

DJ: Would you subscribe to the thought that if the story of baseball is really the story of America, then the story now is one of the decline in standards — both in terms of the play on the field and in terms of the behavior of both the owners and the players?

KB: No, the game is threatened most seriously by television and greed, but those threats, particularly greed, have been along since the beginning. Owners behave the way they've always behaved; players behave the way they've always behaved, with one caveat: the players are more distant from us than they've ever been, and that's a really great threat. That's a product of television and greed. For the first hundred years of the professional game, from 1869 to say 1975 the average baseball player made 8-9 times the salary of a working man. Now he makes 50 times that amount. That puts him far away. And I think that's a scary thing. Because it means the gifted athlete is making a conscious choice to go into baseball not because he loves it but because that's where the money is; a baseball career if you're good at it can last a lot longer than a pro basketball or football career, because of the stress to the body. So I think you're finding players who have absolutely no love of the game, perpetuating some problems.

But having said that, the play has never been better than it is right now; the devotion to the game by the fans is never better. Despite what you may read, attendance is 'way, 'way up, all around. Baseball is in the blood. I think that the parity that we've seen in the last 15 years, particularly in that one 10-year stretch when for the first time in the history of the game ten different teams won the World Series, is a tribute. Most importantly you have last place teams, in the case of Minnesota, winning the Series the next year. That's exactly what

the game should be about.

DJ: Did you discuss in fairly broad terms the aspects of the game, such as the minor leagues, and the amateur leagues, things like the Park League in Boston?

KB: No. We set out to do all that, but as the editing progressed we realized we had enough to swallow in following the broad narrative of the major leagues. We do acknowledge the spirit of the amateur game throughout. We followed the black leagues, and not just in the sense of a tragic Negro Leagues section like a black history month, but throughout every episode. We sowed the seeds and develop this at times very glorious story of a burgeoning black culture in America, and how baseball expressed the exuberance of that culture, and not just the tragic side. We of course acknowledge with fury the unfairness of the segregated leagues, but we don't in any way take a patronizing tone. In fact it's great to see the Monarchs and the Grays and the Crawfords and the Cuban X-Giants.

DJ: The one hero of this program from the press and things that I've read so far appears to be Jackie Robinson standing like a colossus of baseball above the game for his humanity and courage and the example that was put forward. Who are some of the other great heroes of the drama, and are there some heroes that would be unexpected?

KB: I'm sort of excited about showing a complexity to Casey Stengel that I don't think has been there in portraits I've seen before. I look forward to sharing the magnificent drama of Curt Flood and I look forward to adding to Babe Ruth and Ty Cobb, people much understood and much caricatured. And I think the fullness of the portraits that we've done, particularly of Cobb and Ruth, are exciting to me. I'd like to share with you the humor and the outrageousness and the truthfulness of Ted Williams, a side that I don't think has been seen. I think our portrait of Mickey Mantle is really quite good, and I think you'll get to know Rube Waddell and Walter Johnson and Grover Cleveland Alexander in ways you hadn't before. I think

you'll *love* Honus Wagner. I think you'll be shocked by what you find out about Cap Anson, the greatest player of the 19th century. I think you'll finally find out that Abner Doubleday had nothing to do with this game, and at the same time learn a lot about a man named Alexander Joy Cartwright.

DJ: I was very surprised to learn that John McGraw carried a piece of rope from a lynching, was this...?

KB: It was a good luck charm. Yet after his death his wife found among his belongings a list of all the black players he secretly wished to hire over the decades.

DJ: Because he had tried to get...

KB: Charlie Grant.

DJ: He also wanted to get black players by listing them as Cubans and things. He had tried very hard to do that.

KB: When George Bernard Shaw came over to this country and met McGraw he said this is the one true American. To him McGraw epitomized America, and unfortunately he does, in all his fury and his self-determination, in his competitiveness, his anger, his racism, and yet tolerance. McGraw is another one of the people you'll enjoy getting to know.

DJ: Would you say that as a result of the film that you are more connected to the game than ever before?

KB: Absolutely. My philosophy is simple: you can't know where you're going, as a community, as an individual, unless you know where you've been. And where you've been is called history. That's what I'm interested in talking about. So as I've pursued the history of baseball I've enriched my present and I hope made my future a little clearer and brighter.

DJ: Are there plans to broadcast the show internationally? I think it would be wonderful, and beautiful.

KB: Certainly we always we have an agent who peddles it. "The Civil War" played in 35 countries, so we're hoping that people will see "Baseball" as a sequel. In other words, if you're interested in finding out about these curious and complicated people who call themselves Americans then you better take a look at baseball.

DJ: One last question, did you speak to children about who their heroes are in the game and do you think that we're in jeopardy of losing a generation that will be as connected to the game as our generation has been?

KB: We didn't formally speak to them, that is to say on camera. But yes, throughout the production we have talked and it's clear that one of the great threats to the game is television's dictating that World Series games be played at night. So now we have whole generations of people growing up without being able to participate in the glory of that event.

DICK JOHNSON serves as Curator of The Sports Museum of New England in Cambridge, Mass. He is co-author with Glenn Stout of "Ted Williams: A Portrait in Words and Pictures" and is currently working with Stout on "Joe DiMaggio: An Illustrated Life," to be published by Walker And Company in 1995.

Way Out West

By Dick Beverage

AT THE MAJOR LEAGUE meetings in December, 1945, Clarence H. "Pants" Rowland, President of the Pacific Coast League, presented a proposal to a committee of major league executives that he hoped would change the map of major league baseball forever. The PCL requested recognition as a third major league, beginning with the 1946 season. It would no longer be subject to the major league draft and would eventually become a participant in the World Series.

The majors thanked Mr. Rowland and promised to give his proposal very careful study. After an appropriate interval, the request was denied. The Coast League parks were inadequate, they said. Get the ballparks ready and we'll consider you again.

A fateful event in Pacific Coast League history, indeed. For the next eleven years the league continued to advocate its major league status, and in fact, the PCL was elevated to Open Classification, a step above the other minor leagues. But major league status was never forthcoming, and when the major leagues devoured Los Angeles and San Francisco in 1958, the league's aspirations were ended forever.

**RUNS, HITS, AND AN ERA-
THE PACIFIC COAST LEAGUE,
1903-58**
By Paul J. Zingg & Mark D. Medeiros
University of Illinois Press, 1994,
$44.95 hardback; $19.95 paper

NUGGETS ON THE DIAMOND
**Professional Baseball in the Bay
Area from the Gold Rush
to the Present**
By Dick Dobbins and Jon Twichell
Woodford Press, 1994,
$36.95 hardback; $29.95 paper

PACIFIC COAST LEAGUE STARS
**One Hundred of the Best,
1903 - 1957**
By John Spalding
Self published, 1994.
$19.95 hardback; $16.95 paper

The near major league status of the PCL is part of the charm that exists for aficionados of this league, along with its lengthy schedules and geographical isolation for much of its early existence. In recent years interest in the Coast League has revived somewhat, and we've seen an increased number of books and literature on its history. This spring we are blessed with three fine books which cover the subject in depth. Their publication coincided with a museum exhibition of PCL memorabilia and history to bring interest to its highest in forty years. Although the trio cover much of the same ground, they essentially complement each other with the result that our knowledge of the Pacific Coast League and baseball on the West Coast is vastly increased.

"Runs, Hits and an Era" was published in conjunction with the opening of the PCL exhibit at the Oakland Museum and was designed to provide an overview of the display for the museum patrons. It turned out to be much more than that. Paul Zingg was Dean of Liberal Arts at St. Mary's College and had just finished a fine biography of Harry Hooper when he accepted this task, and the tools of the historian are everywhere in evidence. He begins with the origins of baseball in the San Francisco Bay Area in 1859 with the San Francisco Eagles and parallels the develop-

ment of the game in the West with similar events in the East. The events that led to the formation of the Pacific Base Ball League in 1878 and subsequently the California League are well summarized as is the creation of the Pacific Coast League in 1903. Zingg does not confine his view to the baseball field but provides an overlay of the impact of economic and political developments in the United States.

Zingg takes the reader through each decade in similar style — he focuses on the important players and great teams of each era, and we learn much about players who are no more than a footnote in some histories; Ping Bodie, for instance, who was much more than the roommate of Babe Ruth's trunk. His work is augmented by informative sidebars done by Medeiros, who provides information on baseball cards in the PCL, cheerleaders at the ball park, Joe DiMaggio's 61 game hitting game streak and a glimpse of the announcers. The book is heavily illustrated, contains a fine bibliography and index and includes the league standings for each year.

The book is only 148 pages in length, and this limits Zingg's ability to explore certain important issues. He doesn't spend much time on the importance of the freedom from the draft and how it con-

tributed to the fine Seals teams of the '20s nor is he able to give the reader a complete picture of the Depression era. His description of the end of segregation in the PCL during the late '40s is excellent, and he provides a rare look at black baseball on the Pacific Coast. His treatment of the attempt to become a third major league is brief but adequate, and he points out that the insistence of the PCL that all of its cities be elevated to major league status provided the major leagues with a convenient reason for rejection.

One of the sadder days of my early life occurred when I learned that the Oakland Oaks, the first love of my life, were moving to Vancouver. Zingg gives us the usual reasons behind this move — poor attendance, a rotting ballpark, the impact of television on minor league baseball. The Seals were struggling at this same time, and one wonders how anyone could conceive that the Bay Area would support major league baseball. Yet, two years later the Giants were on their way to San Francisco, where they played to capacity crowds at Seals Stadium. Could the Seals/Oaks have done as well if they had worn the major league label? We'll never know.

Zingg's work isn't the full length history of the PCL that the league deserves, but it is the best so far. Complementing his work is "Nuggets on the Diamond," an in-depth look at the baseball teams of the San Francisco Bay Area through 1993. In-depth for only some of the teams, I should say; the Giants and A's merit only ten percent of the 288 pages. But that's just about right for this book. Dick Dobbins is a lifelong resident of the Bay Area and cut his teeth on PCL baseball. He has accumulated an enormous collection of photographs and memorabilia, and we are privileged to see a portion of it here. The pictures alone are worth the price of the book; game action in Recreation Park in 1920, the billboards on the walls of Seals Stadium and a team picture of the San Francisco Pacifics of 1866 are among the treasures you will see, as well as sixteen full pages of memorabilia in color. But Dobbins and Twichell have written a fine book as well.

They begin with a description of game on February 22, 1860 between the Red Rovers and the San Franciscos. The game ended in a 33-33 tie and goes down as the first game ever played in the Bay Area. The authors cover the nineteenth century in a different way than most by devoting a chapter to "Casey at the Bat." It is an appropriate part of the history, after all. Ernest Lawrence Thayer was an employee of the San Francisco Examiner when he wrote

the poem, and it appeared there on June 3, 1888.

By concentrating on the Bay Area the authors are able to develop a topic in more depth, and nowhere is this more apparent than

in their coverage of the decade of the '20s. That was the period when the Seals enjoyed their greatest success with four pennants and two second place finishes, the Oaks were winners and even the Missions enjoyed a successful year with a half championship in the split season of 1929. They correctly link the freedom from the draft to the accumulation of fine talent by Charley Graham and the Seals. Three Hall of Famers trod the Recreation Park outfield in the '20s — Paul Waner, Lloyd Waner and Earl Averill — and each gets his just due. The Depression also gets strong treatment, and the authors insert a chapter on scouting to emphasize

how important local talent became during this period when no club had much money. The inroads of the major league farm systems on Bay Area talent would eventually prove to be fatal for the Pacific Coast League. The local clubs couldn't compete with offers from the major leagues, and inevitably they would be left with the secondary prospects.

If there is one figure who towers over Bay Area baseball, it is Lefty O'Doul. Born in San Francisco in 1897, he pitched and hit for the Seals and after his major league career was over came back to manage his hometown Seals for seventeen years. O'Doul's career is well described here with major attention given to his role as baseball's ambassador to Japan. The important Bay Area families are given their due as well. Naturally, the DiMaggios are the royalty but not far behind are the Raimondis and the Hafeys. The authors give Casey Stengel similar treatment but in an interesting sidebar the tactics of Stengel and Dressen are compared. I'd never seen this comparison before and learned that Charlie doesn't come off badly at all in this rating by one who played for both men.

The authors give great attention to the role of Paul Fagan, the owner of the Seals during the postwar period. It seems clear that his views were more grandiose than any other

magnate, and perhaps frightening as well. Nevertheless, he transformed the Seals into a major league look-alike with travel by air, near major league salaries and a refurbished Seals Stadium. Had the management of other Coast League clubs followed his lead, the league could have achieved major league status before the Invasion, otherwise known as the transfer of the Dodgers and Giants to the West.

If this book has a flaw, it is the lack of a bibliography. Dobbins had access to the private papers of several PCL officials which are an important source for this book. The problem with this approach is that one wonders where he found the information. The inner workings of the PCL meetings during the '20s are not attributed to anyone. Did the author invent these events? A bibliography and proper footnoting would answer these questions.

The third author of this triumvirate takes a completely different approach in "Pacific Coast League Stars." John Spalding is a retired reporter from the San Jose Mercury News and uses his fine reportorial style to give us a capsule history of the PCL through biographies of its players. He selects a group of the most important players from each decade to tell the story of the league. The players are described with their idiosyncrasies and their strengths. You learn why some players with big PCL numbers never did

much in the majors; Fuzzy Hufft had a week glove and was once benched for poor fielding despite hitting .388 at the time. Ox Eckhardt's swing is described, complements of Casey Stengel, "He's almost on top of the plate and when he swings he falls away from it." A photograph accompanies each biography, and for the most part they are great ones. You see babyfaced Tony Freitas, Grumpy Guy Fletcher and Kewpie Dick Barrett. I'd never seen a picture of Paul Strand, but he's right there, in a Portland Beaver uniform. We see Jimmie Reese as a handsome hot prospect with the Oaks in 1927. The players come to life at last. They're no longer just a line of type in "Minor League Stars" or the Reach Guide.

Spalding's book is the kind you take with you to a SABR meeting to start an argument. It's like a Hall of Fame of the PCL. Who should be in there and who shouldn't? Spalding weighs the high averages of the '20s and '30s fairly heavily, and almost half of the players are from those two decades. Ironically, I think he left out some important PCL names of that era, to wit, Fred Haney, Dudley Lee, Carl Ditmar and Mickey Heath. The '50s have only ten representatives, but I wouldn't include Jim Marshall, even though he did play for the

Oaks. Nonetheless, I'm glad to read about each and every one of them.

Where this book is lacking, in my opinion, is an appendix that contains each player's complete playing record. Spalding confines his statistics to a one-line summary of the entire Coast League career and the numbers in what the author considers his best. This approach is a little frustrating, if you want to know what he did year by year. I would also like more information about what happened to each after he left the PCL, and this information is only occasionally included. These are issues of technique. If I'm truly interested, I'll go do the research.

As a PCL buff of long standing, I'm overjoyed to see these three books in print and have learned much from each of them. If you are only casually interested in the PCL, perhaps Zingg and Medeiros will be enough to satisfy you. It is the best single volume on the league to date. However, I predict that once you get started, "betcha can't read just one."

DICK BEVERAGE is founder and president of the Pacific Coast League Historical Society, and author of "The Hollywood Stars" and "The Angels."

Why the Rules Are

By Bill Gilbert

IN THE SEVENTH INNING AT Ebbets Field on August 15, 1926, the bases were loaded with one out in a 1-1 game when Brooklyn rookie Babe Herman lofted a towering fly to deep right field. The runners on second and third tagged up thinking the ball might be caught, but it hit the wall. Hank DeBerry, the man on third, scored but the runner on second, pitcher Dazzy Vance, after rounding third, decided he would be out at the plate and headed back to the bag. The runner on first, Chick Fewster, arrived at third about the same time, but seeing Vance returning, started back toward second. However, before Fewster could get more than a few yards, Herman, with his head down, roared past him and slid into third with what he thought was a bases-clearing triple. The confused Fewster decid-

ed that he might as well add to the logjam at third and for a few seconds the Dodgers had three runners at third base.

When Boston third sacker Eddie Taylor received the ball, he tagged Vance and Herman. Fewster, meanwhile, set sail for second where he was tagged out by second baseman, Doc Gautreau. The three umpires working the game conferred briefly before ruling both Fewster and Herman (for passing Fewster) out. Vance, the lead runner, was the one entitled to the bag. Thus Herman doubled into a double play, although the legend has grown and storytellers frequently relate that Herman tripled into a triple play.

This kind of anecdote is the way author David Nemec elucidates the rules of the game. The book is well organized and includes an appendix which contains the Official Base-

---

THE RULES OF BASEBALL
Illustrated and Explained
By David Nemec
Lyons & Burford, 1994,
203 pp., $16.95

ball Rules (10 sections). The body of the book contains ten chapters, one for each section of the rules. The rules are noted in sidebars within the chapters and are accompanied by narratives discussing the history of the rule and/or an illustration, such as the Herman incident, of the application of the rule. The stories illustrating the rules are well researched and contain appropriate details.

While the basic rules of baseball are remarkably similar to those that existed in the early days, a number of them have evolved over the years due to equipment improvements and other changes. For example, the infield fly rule didn't appear until 1895, a full half century after Alexander Cartwright devised the first formal set of playing rules. In the early days when gloves were more of a protective device than a fielding tool, catching an infield pop-up was far from a sure thing. Further improvements in gloves later triggered another rule change when, in 1954, players could no longer leave their gloves on the field when they came in to bat. The new larger gloves were becoming a tripping hazard. Readers under 50 will probably be shocked to learn that gloves were once left all over the field when players came in to bat.

Many well known events in baseball history serve as illustrations of the rules, including the George Brett pine tar incident, the Nippy Jones shoe polish case and the disallowed hit-by-pitch involving Dick Dietz which preserved Don Drysdale's scoreless inning streak. Orel Hershiser was also the beneficiary of the enforcement of a rule in his quest to break Drysdael's record. Umpire Paul Runge called interference on Brett Butler for sliding out of the baseline to prevent a double play, thus disallowing an apparent run.

The last section in the rules (and therefore the last chapter in the book) deals with the official scorer. Changes in scoring have had an impact on the way the game is played. For example, in 1887, the scoring rules were changed to count bases on balls as hits. Many players then went up to the plate looking for walks causing some games to drag out for over two hours. (Imagine that!) The new rule was scrapped after a one-season trial.

One scoring standard that has changed several times is eligibility for the batting title. In 1954, Ted Williams batted .345 with over 520 plate appearances. However, the batting title was awarded to Bobby Avila who hit .341 because Williams failed to meet the then-existing standard of 2.6 at bats times the number of games played by the team. Boston played 156 games in 1954 requiring Williams

to have 406 at-bats to qualify. But along with his 386 at-bats Williams landed 136 walks. In 1957, the rule was changed to require 3.1 plate appearances per game played and it remains that way today (502 plate appearances in a 162-game season).

Before 1951, the standard for a pitcher to qualify for the ERA title was 10 complete games. If that rule were still in effect, there would have been no qualifiers in the National League in 1993 and only four in the American League. The rule was changed in 1951 to require a pitcher to pitch as many innings as the number of games played by the club. This change was made primarily to give relief pitchers an opportunity to qualify. In 1952, when the season consisted of 154 games, Hoyt Wilhelm won the National League ERA title with a 2.43 ERA in 159 innings, all in relief.

While Nemec's book is well written and provides a useful reference source, it may not appeal to a large segment of the baseball-reading population. Knowledgeable fans are generally familiar with the rules and have probably heard most of the stories Nemec uses to embellish them. Casual fans may find that there is much more here than they ever wanted to know about the rules. For myself, it will be a useful addition to my baseball library alongside one of Nemec's earlier books, "Great Baseball Feats, Facts and Firsts."

The book is being published in cooperation with Major League Baseball. As an Official Publication of Major League Baseball, it will carry the familiar ball-and-batter logo of the Major Leagues.

BILL GILBERT, a chemical engineer retired from Exxon, is a lifelong baseball fan and an active member of SABR, who now spends much of his time writing about baseball for various publications.

They Invented 'Inside Baseball'

By Eric London

1994 is the most significant anniversary year in the history of the Baltimore Orioles. It is the fortieth anniversary year for the present Orioles, formerly the hapless St. Louis Browns. Bird-watchers have good reason to celebrate: what was one of the worst franchises in major league history from 1902 to 1953 became one of the very best. Since divisional play began, only the Oakland A's have made more trips to the World Series (six) than the Orioles (five), tied with Cincinnati.

But there is another anniversary which will not receive as much notice, yet which should be of equal note. 1994 is the one-hundredth anniversary of one of the most talented and exciting baseball teams of all-time — the 1894 National League Champion Baltimore Orioles. While the 1894 team does not share a direct bloodline with the present-day Birds — they dropped out of the National League after the 1899 season — the 1994 version plays in a city which developed its affinity for baseball from watching and cheering the rugged bunch known as "Hanlon's O's."

Unfortunately, a near total lack of attention has been paid to the 1894 team by contemporary baseball writers. Almost all coverage of the team has been limited to brief mentions in biographies of John McGraw — biographies which almost solely focus on McGraw's later career as the manager of the New York Giants. Standing alone in exclusive coverage is Robert W. Creamer's wonderful essay "The Old Orioles" in "The Ultimate Baseball Book."

According to Creamer, his generation, the generation which grew

up during the Great Depression and which came of age during World War II, was raised in the belief that the 1894 Orioles were one of the best teams, if not the best team in history. Although he confesses to not knowing why he persisted in this belief as a child, he seems to have convinced himself of this as an adult in writing his fine essay.

Creamer states that "[l]egend said they were the greatest team of all time until the 1927 Yankees came along." While he discounts John McGraw's claim that the Old Orioles were better than the Yanks, and puts more credence into Wilbert Robinson's that the legendary Yanks "would have beat our brains out," he makes a strong case that both teams should at least be mentioned in the same breath.

One thing is undeniable: both teams towered over all pre-World War II clubs in terms of talent and influence. The 1927 Yankees had six future Hall of Famers: Earle Combs, Lou Gehrig, Waite Hoyt, Tony Lazzeri, Herb Pennock and Babe Ruth. So did the 1894 Orioles: catcher Wilbert Robinson, first baseman Dan Brouthers, shortstop Hughie Jennings, third baseman John "Muggsy" McGraw (voted in the Hall as a manager), left fielder Joe Kelley, and right fielder "Wee" Willie Keeler. The Yankees gave us "Murderers Row"; the Orioles gave us "the Baltimore chop," "hit 'em where they ain't," and "inside baseball."

Even if one gives the talent edge to the Yankees, the Orioles were a more colorful team, and certainly there has never been a meaner diamond nine in professional baseball history. They were real Baltimore toughs, as McGraw reminisced: "[w]e'd spit tobacco juice on a spike wound, rub dirt in it, and get out there and play."

They also played fast and loose with the rules whenever they could get away with it. Creamer recalls the stories he read as a child about the legendary Orioles: "how they'd scuff up a baseball or discolor it with tobacco juice to help their pitchers; how they'd cut corners running from first to third when the umpire's back was turned; how they'd hold a base runner's belt to delay his departure from a base."

Creamer's recollections aren't far from the truth. An article from The Sporting News dated April 14, 1894 titled "Tough McGraw: His

Disreputable Actions on the Ball Field at New Orleans" condemns his actions as the Orioles' ringleader with the harshest language:

It is known in every city where McGraw has played that is he a rough, unruly man who is constantly playing dirty ball. He has the vilest tongue of any ball player... While McGraw is a fine ball player, yet he adopts every low and contemptible method that his erratic brain can conceive to win a play by a dirty trick.

McGraw wasn't the sole offender. Charles Alexander, in his scholarly biography "John McGraw," quotes Tim Murnane, a Boston baseball writer of the time, as saying the O's played "the dirtiest ball ever seen in this country." They were ready to "maim a fellow player for life [in] just retribution for trying to stop them in their temporary flight." Their tactics: "diving into the first baseman long after he has caught the ball; throwing masks in front of the runners at home plate; catching them by the clothes at the first base and interfering with the catcher."

But they didn't win with a lack of hustle: Creamer also talks about how they developed "inside baseball," "the tight, close to the vest brand of ball that stretched out a run or two and then protected it with strong pitching and deft fielding." It was a new and revolutionary style of playing. New York Times writer Joseph Durso in his biography "The Days of Mr. McGraw" quotes the New York Giants manager of that era, John Montgomery Ward, as saying "[t]hat isn't baseball the Orioles are playing. It's an entirely new game."

Their talent was impeccable. McGraw, no mean judge of talent, said that "[w]ith the possible exception of Ty Cobb, Willie Keeler was the greatest player of all time..." Creamer describes Joe Kelley as "one of the greatest, if not the greatest, of the Old Orioles." His statistics bear this out. According to Creamer, from 1894 through 1898, he averaged .360, hit with power, stole bases, scored runs, fielded well, and didn't miss a game four straight seasons. Creamer adds that during that same period, Hughie Jennings "was one of the best shortstops that ever lived."

But it wasn't just the incredible talent which led the team to the pennant. They also had one of the finest managers of the day: Ned Hanlon. Hanlon became manager in 1892, taking over a team that had just finished in last place in the twelve team National League, 54-1/2 games out of first behind the Boston Beaneaters. Hanlon set out to take control of the team both on and off the field. Within a year, he had obtained a thirty-percent interest in the club and persuaded Harry Von der Horst, the club president, to step aside and let him function as both manager and president of the team.

The Orioles showed immediate results under Hanlon's leadership. They went from 55 games under .500 in 1992 to 10 games under in 93. Still, they finished 26-1/2 games behind Boston, eighth in a twelve team league. However, the attendance doubled and the franchise showed a profit for the first time since the 1880s.

Hanlon's primary contribution to the team was his ability to put together a team with six future Hall of Famers in two years. The only players who stayed from the team he took over were McGraw, Robinson, and pitcher Sadie McMahon. Hanlon quickly assembled, through skill and foresight, a team which shot from last to first in two short seasons. He picked up young unknowns Kelley, Jennings, and Keeler and the seemingly washed-up Brouthers in trades, giving away tested and talented veterans for young unknowns.

In 1894, the Orioles were at best seen as a long shot to capture the flag. The Sporting News weekly baseball column "Caught on The Fly" stated on May 12 that "the Baltimores are considered the 'dark horse' in the League race this season." This was said after the team was already on its way to the pennant, winning 24 of its first 34 games. The team went on to win 34 of their first 47, sneaking into first place past Pittsburgh and Cleveland. Commenting on the good fortune of the team after the first leg of the season, TSN stated simply on June 9 that "Hanlon is happy."

The Orioles held onto first place through June and July, and began to slip behind Boston in the standings towards the end of the month. By August, the Orioles collapsed, falling far behind Boston. TSN was

quick to write Baltimore off on August 4: "Boston is setting the pace and the Orioles lost every game played last week and seem to have gone to pieces." By the 11th, TSN sarcastically commented that "the sweet scented Orioles must commence hustling once more or they will be left."

According to Creamer, it was Hanlon's radical shift of McGraw from leadoff to cleanup position in the order which saved the day. Whatever the reason, the Oriole bats exploded, and by the end of August, they were almost back in first. However, the bad boys still had not convinced the baseball establishment that they wouldn't choke. On August 25, TSN commented on their comeback attempt: "[t]he splendid team has been the surprise of the season — that is the way it has held up in the top notch." But the columnist added it was dubious whether they could hold out: "This team may show an ability to win on the last western trip which will enable it to beat out the present champions. But I am rather inclined to doubt it."

The O's proved everyone wrong. They continued on their tear, causing TSN to issue a correction on September 8: "the many predictions that the Orioles would drop before now are proving incorrect." By September 15, TSN declared that "there is yet a possibility that either Boston or New York will beat out the Marylanders, but it is a remote one." The Orioles won 28 of their last 31 games, and clinched the pennant in a victory in Cleveland against Cy Young. They ended the season three games in front of New York in the standings.

They won on their hitting and running, not their pitching. Six of their eight starters hit .335 or better; in the stealing category, Jennings had 36, Kelley 45, Brodie 50, and McGraw 77. And they led the League in on-base percentage at .418, 45 points over the League average, a season team record which has never been duplicated in the history of organized baseball.

The post-season play of the '94 team was an anticlimax, the Orioles losing to the Giants 4-0 in an unnoteworthy series. In one of those strange twists of fate, the 1894 series was the only time a team

with a winning percentage as high as the Orioles' (.695) went winless in post-season play until the 111-game winning Cleveland Indians (.721) dropped four in a row, also to the New York Giants.

As there was only one league in existence in 1894, the ex- president of the Pittsburgh team, William Chase Temple, humbly established a postseason best-of-seven contest between the first-and second-place teams in the National League to be played for the Temple Cup. An interesting history of pre-1903 postseason play, including all four Temple Cup series, can be found in "Glory Fades Away" by Jerry Lansche. Lansche is a great defender of the proposition that the Nineteenth-Century World Series were on a par with the Twentieth-Century contests, a dubious proposition. However, the Temple Cup did not even have the advantage of other pre-1903 world series where teams from rival leagues played each other for the first time in the season.

In the eyes of many observers, especially in Baltimore, all the Cup did was to belittle the achievement of the Orioles regular-season, pennant-winning performance. The discontentment was not solely Baltimorean sour grapes; Nick Young, President of the National League, stated: "the Baltimores won the championship fairly and squarely and cleanly and they are the real champions." And in TSN, the Boston correspondent, writing under the pseudonym "Bean Blower", added that "surely nothing of a championship nature was gained by the New Yorks in the series." He added that "you can count on the New York press to withhold anything if it is a possible thing to do, but to deprive the Baltimore club of anything that belongs to the honor of securing a National League pennant will be out of the question." It is ironic that the "new" wild-card playoff format in 1994 will pit a second place team against a first place team — much like the discredited Temple Cup a century ago. The first time a wild-card team beats the first place team in their division in the expanded playoff format, I suspect the new format will go the way of the Temple Cup, which was eliminated after four years due to lack of fan interest.

Creamer states that unlike the Yankees of 1927, the 1894 Orioles "were not a dynasty at all but a nova, a sudden manifestation in the baseball skies that flared brilliantly for a very short time and then disappeared." Even if one cedes this point to Creamer, (I do not — a team that from 1894-98 finished first three times, second twice, and had an overall winning percentage of .680 and played in every post-season tournament held during those years surely qualifies as a dynasty), Muggsy and Ned's fiery Old Orioles are every bit as worthy of celebrating this year as are Brooksie, Frank and Rip's forty-year old Birds.

Discussed in this article:

"The Old Orioles" by Robert W. Creamer, from "The Ultimate Baseball Book," edited by Daniel Okrent and Harris Lewine with historical text by David Nemec, Houghton Mifflin Company, Boston, 1984, 352 pp., $15.95.

"Glory Fades Away: The Nineteenth-Century World Series Rediscovered" by Jerry Lansche, Taylor Publishing, Dallas, 1991, 328 pp., $19.95.

"John McGraw" by Charles C. Alexander, Viking, New York, 1988, 358 pp, $19.95.

"The Days of Mr. McGraw," republished in "Casey & Mr. McGraw" by Joseph Durso, The Sporting News, St. Louis, 1989, 367 pp., $19.95.

The Sporting News, April-October 1894, St. Louis.

ERIC LONDON currently lives in Washington, D.C., ten blocks from Griffith Stadium and forty minutes from Camden Yards.

'The Man' Never Showed

By Jack Carlson

WHO WAS STAN Musial? He is "The Man" who seemingly everyone (with the possible exception of opposing pitchers) liked. He is "The Man" who played major league baseball for 22 years and lost one year while he served in the Armed Forces. He is "The Man" who set 17 major league records, 19 National League records, and nine All-Star Game records.

Most baseball enthusiasts know that Musial began his pro career as a pitcher until an arm injury forced him off the mound and into the outfield. How many know that he returned to his last year of high school after his first pro season? How many know that he worked in his father-in-law's grocery store after his second professional baseball season and in the Donora (Pa.)

____
STAN THE MAN MUSIAL:
Born to be a Ballplayer
By Jerry Lansche
Taylor, 1994, 212 pp., $19.95
____

zinc works after playing in the 1942 season?

When Musial began playing baseball, the conditions were unbelievably different from those experienced by today's players. Can anyone imagine one of today's players who had already won two MVP awards hitch-hiking? Musial did that, going from Philadelphia to Donora after being discharged from the Navy. Late in his career he was benched from time to time. Musial did not pose and posture for the media and complain about "no respect." He did not proclaim his greatness. He was a team-first, not a me-first, man.

Just how good was Stanley Frank Musial? Let's compare him to one of today's acclaimed superstars — one who many say is baseball's best player (a star who one expert recently said is better than Ted

Williams): Barry Bonds.

There are some similarities between Bonds and Musial. Each was 21 at the start of his first full major league season. Each batted lefthanded and played mostly left

A particularly good chapter describes the 1947 season and dwells on Jackie Robinson's entry into the major leagues.

field in his early career. Each won three MVPs in his first eight seasons. So let's compare Bonds' and Musial's first eight seasons.

From years 1 through 8, Musial played in 37 more games than Bonds but batted more than 500 more times. Musial scored more than 100 more runs than Bonds, and rang up 81 more doubles, and 75 more triples. Barry outhomered Stan the Man by 49, but Musial knocked in 129 more runs. In total bases Musial cranked up 523 more. Bonds landed almost 90 more walks than Musial, but Barry fanned almost three times as much.

Here are batting, slugging and on-base averages for each: Bonds, .283, .526, .391; Musial, .346, .580, .426.

How do these achievements compare to the contemporaries of each? Well, in his first nine seasons Musial led his league in hits, doubles and slugging average five times; in batting, triples, total bases and on-base average four times; in runs twice and homers once. Mr. Bonds has three times led his league in on-base average, twice in slugging, once each in homers, RBIs and total bases.

Readers may draw their own conclusions. The most money Stan Musial ever made in his career was $100,000. Today he might be worth a hundred times that.

Author Lansche's biography is the most recent of at least four earlier Musial bios, including two autobiographical works. The author describes Musial's life from his Donora childhood through 1963, which was Stan's last year in baseball. There is a factual and statistical presentation of each season. Stan's personal life is described in terms of family events and outside or non-baseball businesses. It's all here: Musial's triumphs and his struggles. The latter are pretty much concentrated in the beginning and at the end of his career.

A reviewer must ask where the author of a biography obtains his information. For a subject still living, it may be the subject himself or intimate friends, family, business

associates, etc. In other cases, letters or writing of either the subject or others may be used. In this book, the information sources are not clear. There are no references nor bibliography. Where did the author obtain the necessary information? If not from Musial, and there is certainly no indication of Musial's participation, what are the sources?

Musial's first autobiography appeared in 1964, shortly after his retirement from the game, and his collaborator was long-time St. Louis baseball writer Bob Broeg. The early portion of "Stan The Man Musial" appears to borrow extensively from the Musial/Broeg book. There is nothing wrong with that if proper attribution is given. In this case it is not.

Despite all that, this is an interesting book which provides the reader with the sense of Musial's career. His year-by-year activities are faithfully chronicled although there is no attempt to get inside the man to tell why he was so modest and seemingly without ego. Perhaps it was a wonderful self-confidence or it may be that Musial is a modest man whose deeds proclaimed his greatness, and in his era (unlike today) bombast was somehow just plain impolite.

Now, more than 30 years after Musial's retirement, it is time to probe more deeply into personality and motivation. The baseball career has been well chronicled not only in this book but in others published previously in addition to many articles. (The Musial listings in Myron Smith's "Baseball Bibliography" take up nearly three full pages.)

But questions remain. For example, during the 1946 season, Musial was moved from left field to first base. The author doesn't mention it until a casual comment at chapter's end. Why was Musial moved? It wasn't a matter of age; Musial was just 25. And he certainly wasn't getting pushed out of the pasture; only one Card outfielder appeared in more than 100 games that year. What did Musial think about the move? Was it difficult to adjust? This was a major event and an opportunity to provide some insight into Musial's thoughts and feelings.

Baseball aficionados may be upset by several careless errors that good editing would have prevented. A reference to Billy Herman as a Dodger outfielder swings and misses. Herman played in 1922, batted .488 as a Dodger, and never played the outfield. When Musial set a National League consecutive games played record in 1954, the author states that the old record had been set by "Chicago catcher Gus Suhr." Suhr never played for Chicago, and never caught. Besides, who ever heard of a catcher setting a consec-

utive game record?

A particularly good chapter in Lansche's book describes the 1947 season and dwells on Jackie Robinson's entry into the major leagues. Here the author provides a good description of the Cardinal players' reactions and present some opinions and conclusions of his own. Would that there were more of that type of presentation throughout the book.

This book maybe viewed as an opportunity lost. New ground is there to be explored. The sources are still available (but for how long?). Instead of another career review, there could have been much more. We wish and hope for something new and penetrating and that yet remains to be done.

JACK CARLSON saw his first Pirate game sixty years ago. He has played baseball in McKeesport, Pa., on the same field once graced by Musial.

Long Tall Texan

By Eliot Cohen

LAMENTING HIS COUNTRY'S underdeveloped baseball skills, a French sportswriter complained, "We have pitchers who can scratch and spit like John Wayne, but whose windup is shaky." That 1991 statement demonstrated the transoceanic influence of Nolan Ryan, called John Wayne in spikes by more than one American scribe.

The cowboy image fits Ryan, the off-season cattle rancher and fastest gun on the mound who spent his most productive seasons playing for the two Texas teams and the one owned by The Singin' Cowboy, Gene Autry. With his record 27 seasons in the majors, seven no-hitters, 5714 strikeouts and 324 wins, Ryan's reach extends far beyond that great American cowboy image. In "The Meaning of Nolan Ryan,"

THE MEANING OF NOLAN RYAN
By Nick Trujillo
Texas A&M University Press, 163 pp.,
$27.50 cloth, $13.95 paper

---

communications studies professor Nick Trujillo proposes to explore the various images of Ryan to find their significance in the American psyche. It is a partial success.

The book's first 50 pages make a promising start. Recalling the academic revisionist classic, "Joe DiMaggio: A Bio-Bibliography" by Jack B. Moore, Trujillo recounts the highlights of Ryan's career. However, Trujillo's view is skewed. This book grew out of a study of the Texas Rangers franchise while he was teaching at Southern Methodist University in Dallas, and his recap of Ryan's career is far too Ranger-centric, especially considering Ryan spent five years, less than a fifth of his career, with Texas. Ryan's 5000th strikeout (according to book, the victim was a Rickie [sic] Henderson) and 300th win are recounted ad nauseam, as are his

sixth and seventh no-hitters. Strikeout 3509 to break Walter Johnson's record — that stood for six decades — Ryan's 4000th K (you won't find the name of New York Met outfielder Danny Heep, the ex-Astro the ex-Met whiffed), the single season record of 383 strikeouts, and the fifth no-hitter are barely mentioned, though each represented an unprecedented breakthrough. Trujillo can argue those events paled in comparison to the media blitz which followed Ryan's move to Arlington Stadium.

Trujillo explains the Rangers exploited Ryan as a quintessentially Texan figure in a way the Astros did not. Before Ryan arrived, the transplanted Washington Senators were a unappealing footnote, bridging the gap between the most important local sports seasons, football and spring football. Ryan gave the team image and appeal it had lacked during nearly two decades in the Dallas-Fort Worth area. By the time Ryan called it quits after the 1993 season, the Rangers had increased attendance by nearly 50 percent and won a new stadium from local taxpayers, bound to swell attendance further. The Houston Astros, Ryan's hometown team that let him get away, were reduced to a footnote, and owner John McMullen was forced to sell.

Ryan the cowboy is an obvious and fitting image for this solitary gunslinger on the mound and off-season rancher. However, that image was with Ryan long before he arrived in Arlington. Trujillo tries, but fails, to expand our understanding of Ryan's grip on the American imagination. He does provide a number of interesting details, such as the clause in Ryan's personal services contract with Texas which requires him to wear a Rangers hat on his Hall of Fame plaque and an accounting of Ryan's commercial endorsement bonanza. Those details fail to coalesce into a meaningful story.

Instead, readers must settle for the social science habit of naming an observation (re-stating it, and citing colleagues and their names for related observations), rather than offering insight into the reasons behind the facts. We get a discussion of Ryan as a sex symbol, complete with strained examples of phallic symbolism and obligatory denunciations of male dominance in athletic imagery. In a similar wrongheaded but politically correct vein, the media is portrayed as a white, male, middle-aged monolith which distorted the Ryan image to suit its agenda. Those distortions do not, however, disqualify some very white, male, middle-aged media members from citation when their words suit Trujillo's purposes. This academic bent leads to both banal generalities and obscure classical

references far removed from Ryan himself.

Repeated references to Ryan's impact substitute poorly for analysis. Trujillo fails to provide details, save an oft-cited Ryan poster displayed over the stadium entrance, about how the Rangers cashed in on Ryan where the Astros did not. The team's efforts were aided because they are the oldest team without a title of any kind to their credit and there wasn't much else on Texas to crow about, save chatty Dodgerphile manager Bobby Valentine (instead of taking his current job with the Reds, Bobby V. should've answered his calling as the new voice of Kermit the Frog). The phrase, "Nolie follows his own program," was an oft-repeated phrase around the Rangers. Trujillo refers briefly to the special treatment the Rangers gave Ryan and discontent it bred among some teammates, though he doesn't detail the road trips Ryan was allowed to skip, Ranger efforts to start Ryan at home as much as possible, and other privileges he enjoyed. The Sporting News was embarrassed when it published a photo from the Ranger opening day contest at Camden Yards in 1993, purporting to show Ryan in uniform. Ryan had skipped that road trip to prepare for pitching the home opener.

Trujillo might have investigated whether, and if so how, other teams can boost their own stars using the techniques the Rangers developed to exploit Ryan. (Public Relations Director John Blake and staff receive far too little credit for their role in preparing the Ryan strikeout list which kicked Ryan's achievements up to mythic proportions.) Nor does Trujillo explain why the Rangers had failed so miserably to capture the market before Ryan's arrival. Furthermore, as a media expert, it would seem natural for Trujillo to offer some concrete numbers on Ryan's impact, such as newspaper lines, local television ratings or minutes of Ranger coverage on news broadcasts before and after his coming; he does not.

Even at the height of Ryan's exposure and appeal, many analysts cited baseball's lack of national heroes. Did Ryan fail to meet the challenge, or was there simply not enough of Ryan to go around? Admittedly this area is highly speculative, and perhaps of limited interest. It seems to be the ground Trujillo seeks, but he has as much trouble zeroing in on it as batters had with the Ryan Express.

Trujillo goes beyond image to take a stab at rating Ryan the mound performer, but also with limited results. He accepts the media judgment that Ryan's 300th victory erased doubts about his greatness, silencing critics who

called him a .500 pitcher. However, Ryan's 300th win no more made him a great pitcher than Dave Kingman's 400th home run made him a great slugger. Trujillo acknowledges strikeout number

---

For a country that elected another John Wayne substitute as President, Ryan naturally filled the gap.

5000 was a media event rather than a meaningful moment, yet hurdling this other artificial barrier is imbued with almost mystical significance.

That's a judgment Trujillo shares with many alleged baseball experts. However, Trujillo's lack of baseball news is highlighted when he discusses Ryan's seventh no-hitter stealing the spotlight from the all time basestealing record set earlier that day by that "Rickie" Henderson. "Raphael" Palmeiro is cited as one Texas teammate protesting Ryan's special status and privileges. A quote from another source about Ryan's minor league career with the Jacksonville "Sons" offers grounds for an academic investigation as well as inadvertent tribute to a spiritual Star Trek episode. Popular culture is not a Trujillo strength either (not good news for a communications studies professor), judging from his reference to rock musician "Jimmy Hendricks," perhaps a relative of Joggin' George.

Since Trujillo doesn't nail down the meaning of Ryan, I'll try. Ryan's popularity is natural, given that he was always box office boffo, from his days soaking his fingers in pickle brine to combat blisters to using Robin Ventura's head as conga drum. As for pitching greatness, another Texan, Roger Clemens in his prime was the hurler Ryan's fans wish The Express had been. Ryan averaged slightly more than a game a season above .500 for his 27 year career, won 20 games only twice, and lost more games in the twentieth century than any pitcher. He was the hurler people might most want to watch, the most spectacular, the top attraction, but never the one any manager would pray to have on the hill in a must-win game. Ryan was the pitcher most likely to give up a run without any batter making hard contact, given his career records for walks, wild pitches and errors. Though Ryan dismissed his strikeouts as a product of his "pitching style," many rivals believe he was obsessed with the strikeout and encouraged to pile up whiffs by front office types.

Ryan's appeal grew after his arrival in Texas in part because the Rangers were hungry for a hero and tried to make him one. Ryan cooperated with a major league leading 301 strikeouts at age 42 in his first season with the Rangers, then a year later threw his sixth no-hitter. For millions of baby boomers fighting middle age, Ryan offered an example of a guy losing his hair and, despite his rigorous workout program, broadening around the middle, yet winning the battle against advancing years.

Along with sociology, Ryan added a political dimension. Overtly Republican, Ryan's endorsement of a GOP candidate for Texas Agriculture Commissioner threatened Democratic legislative approval of naming the Nolan Ryan Expressway. For a country that elected another John Wayne substitute as President, Ryan naturally filled the gap. Another, less genuine Texan did not after Ronald Reagan left the stage. Ryan embodied admirable Republican values of hard work, family, and cowboy independence. He also embodied annoying Reagan revolution qualities. Ryan was a rich person preaching the value of enjoying life without money, an individual rights advocate playing in a government subsidized stadium, ranching on government subsidized land and criticizing other people's private lives, a participant in his own rampant commercialization, and sufficiently insensitive to use the loaded term "genetics" to explain his pitching longevity.

Along with his golden arm and his 53 major league records, Ryan's presence in the right place at the right time may be a historical accident which can never recur. However, his greatest lasting impact, his deepest meaning, catches Trujillo looking, as if it were a Ryan curve on 3-2. Along with Steve Carlton, his career strikeout rival in the mid-1980s, Ryan's success and longevity validated strenuous conditioning programs for pitchers. Just watching Ryan's workouts, involving hundreds of pounds of weights and thousands of strokes on a stationary bike, was exhausting. Before Carlton and Ryan, pitchers took leisurely runs, threw hard once between starts, and avoided even lifting a suitcase with their money arms. That pair of 300-game winners changed it all. With every hunk of iron they pump, pitchers pay tribute to Ryan's legacy.

ELIOT COHEN edits Who's Who In Baseball and contributes to many baseball publications.

Not Just Guy Stuff

By Steve Gietschier

I N THE ACKNOWLEDGMENTS TO this fine new book, Robert Mayer — you may remember him from "The Grace of Shortstops" — thanks seven of his friends "who graciously allowed me to usurp a part of their lives." These friends are all men and so, when Mayer writes about how baseball has affected the lot of them, himself included, he is indeed writing about baseball and men's lives. Nothing wrong with that. And yet, Mayer's title unsettles me, and maybe it unsettles you, too. Without verging anywhere near the debate over political correctness, perhaps these three bold facts can explain the unease that we feel.

First, Mayer opens his text with an epigram from Annie Dillard. She is obviously one of his favorite writers and a baseball fan besides. She understands the game as he

BASEBALL AND MEN'S LIVES:
The True Confessions of a
Skinny-Marink
By Robert Mayer
Delta Trade Paperbacks, 1994, $12.95

understands the game. Second, Mayer's first wife, Carol, whom he got to know well in a celebration following the World Series triumph of the 1969 Mets, is as deep and profound a fan as he is. And third, Mayer's book makes its debut just as a superior anthology of women writing on baseball, "Diamonds Are a Girl's Best Friend," makes its appearance. [Reviewed on page 197.] So maybe "Baseball and *Our* Lives" might have been a better title choice.

On the other hand, young girls devoted to baseball come to the realization that they will not make the majors in a different way from young boys. Girls face the seemingly insurmountable gender barrier; that's plenty tough. But boys have to face the obstacle that "You're just not good enough." This blow, I think, is a ton-of-bricks, guy kind of

thing. Maybe we should concede this difference to Mayer and accept that it is this encounter with grim reality and the refusal ever to accept it and the fantasizing to reverse it, even into middle age, that cause most men to keep a ball and glove close by, always at the ready, just in case.

Surely not every boy who dreamed of making the majors grew up a Dodger fan. But it does seem that an inordinate number of these lost boys of summer has committed the details of their rites of passage to print. Mayer was the odd Dodger fan who grew up in the Bronx, and it was his older brother who burst young Robert's major league bubble. But even earlier, he had been branded by his mother as a hopeless "skinny-marink." Nobody in the Greater New York Metropolitan Area (as it was then called) knew exactly how this word was spelled or where it came from — one of Mayer's friends admitted to being a "skinny-bolick," and I, for what it's worth, was a "skinny-malink" — but everyone knew what it meant. Playing major league baseball was definitely not part of the term's definition. (Younger students of the vernacular might try on "wuss" as a Generation X equivalent.)

The questions that Mayer, the non-major leaguer, grapples with are, therefore, the same questions we have all toyed with at one point or another: If baseball does not love

us enough to let us play, why do we love it? What does it mean to be a fan? Exactly for whom or what are we rooting? What happens to our loyalty when a team moves or when we move and an expansion team

<hr>

My Ohio-raised wife, who knows her way around the infield fly rule as well as most, was in love with Johnny Bench...

<hr>

erupts nearby? And how do we live the baseball life (i.e., watching, reading, playing, coaching, thinking) when others close to us would rather be tending a garden?

I think Mayer would agree that the best thing about these questions is that they have no definite answers and that real fans, even skinny-marinks, can discuss them at length with great passion. Thus, in this extended essay, they are batted about frequently as Mayer unfolds his personal odyssey, which begins with his first baseball memory in 1946 and ends as Dwight Gooden throws his first pitch of 1993 to Eric Young of the Colorado Rockies.

Making the jump from fan of the

Brooklyn Dodgers to fan of the New York Mets was easy for Mayer and lots of others. Ask anyone who thinks the three greatest villains of the twentieth century were Hitler, Mussolini, and Walter O'Malley. After all, the Dodgers left us; we didn't leave them. But by the time Denver was awarded a franchise, Mayer had long since departed New York for Santa Fe, and his cable-ready Mets were not exactly a team that compelled long-distance devotion. How Mayer works out the dilemma of dealing with this infatuation is beautiful to watch.

Still though, a word needs to be added for those whose baseball lineage is matriarchal as well as patriarchal. In my own case, my father was a devoted Dodger fan, and so was my maternal grandmother. She was the one who learned the game listening to Red Barber, and her detailed notebooks of seasons past are the most treasured part of my inheritance. My Ohio-raised wife, who knows her way around the infield fly rule as well as most, was in love with Johnny Bench before Gary Carter turned her head for a while. Now, we have passed it all on to our girls who diligently adjust the refrigerator magnets on the standings board. Yes, that's right, fathers playing catch with daughters. Baseball and *our* lives, indeed.

STEVE GIETSCHIER is the archivist for The Sporting News.

Ralph Henry Barbour's World of Privilege

By Philip Bergen

OUT BY SECOND, JACK, ON HIS TOES, *alert and ready for anything, heard the crack of bat against ball, and instinctively ran toward base. Hopkins, head down, started like a flash toward third. Then Jack's eyes found the ball. It was speeding toward him, straight, swift and well over his head. He stopped in his tracks a foot or two behind the base-line, threw his hands high into the air, put his weight on to his toes, and then sprang straight upward until there was a good two feet between him and the turf. To the excited watchers it seemed that for an instant he hung there suspended, a lithe, slim figure against the golden sunset haze. Then the ball stung his hands, the throng broke into confused shouting, and —*
"Back! Back!" shrieked the coaches.The runners turned in their tracks and scuttled for the bases they had left like rabbits for their burrows. Jack, the ball securely clutched, reached second in two strides, and then, with a lightning survey of the situation, threw straight and sure to Billings at third. Condit, arrested ten feet from the plate by the coaches' warnings, had doubled back, and now was racing desperately for third base and safety. Six feet from the bag he launched himself forward, arms outstretched. A trailing cloud of red dust arose into the still air, and the ball thumped into the

baseman's hands. The little fat umpire swung his hand circling toward the bases.

"Game!" he said.

WEATHERBY'S INNING (1903)

"I HAVE A YOUNGSTER AT HOME; HE ISN'T VERY BIG yet - just put on his first pair of trousers the other day - but he looks a great deal like a football man already. Some day I expect he'll come here to school. If he does I hope he will row on the crew and play on the eleven or nine, and, if he can, run well or leap the hurdles. But if I had my way I'd fix his victories and defeats for him in a proportion of one victory to nine defeats. For it isn't winning that helps a fellow get a good hard grip on the world, but losing. Yes, fellows, a boy or a man will learn more wisdom - good, useful, every-day wisdom - in one defeat than he will in nine victories. It would be a hard course for Remsen, Jr., but it would make a better man out of him in the end than would a whole eight years of first prizes. So don't despise defeat, as long as it is honorable. Learn to make the most of it. Don't feel down-hearted for more than two minutes and a half; that's quite long enough for regrets. Cheer the victors, and go back and try again. Don't blame the other man because he won -- it was probably your own fault; but shake hands with him and, if you must, tell him to look out for his laurels next time. Defeat ought to teach us courage, perseverance, manliness, good temper, and self-possession — all good things to learn."

FOR THE HONOR OF THE SCHOOL (1900)

IT WAS A SIMPLER TIME, AN ERA FREE OF FREE AGENTS, arbitrarily without arbitration, unencumbered by extensive media coverage, games of the week, autographs as a business and restless franchises. Baseball during the early period of the twentieth century was a pastime enjoyed by much of the nation as participants and spectators — but not so much as readers. Virtually all baseball writing existed as news accounts, concerned with day to day activities; but precious little of what we take for granted today in background pieces, news from other cities and statistics was available. Among the most neglected segments of readers at that time were children.

To be sure there were the Frank Merriwell stories and other imitators, but these were so fanciful as to be shams, filled with routine der-

ring-do, unlikely plots and a distinct lack of respect for their audience and its knowledge. Dime novels appealed to the lowest common denominator among their readers, were temporary fixes, and were recognized as such. What was lacking was an intelligent juvenile writer whose books were exciting, full of realistic baseball action, and able to teach impressionable readers lessons of fair play and sportsmanship. Ralph Henry Barbour, as much as any one author, helped change juvenile sports fiction for the better, and permanently created a niche for books aimed at adolescents.

Today Barbour's works are hard to find, not having been reprinted from the early part of this century, and while he is sometimes recognized by students of baseball literature, his contributions are frequently denigrated and dismissed as antique period pieces.

Yet the man could write — not only often but well! Barbour was born in Cambridge, Massachusetts, in 1870 and worked as a newspaperman out west (he never went to college) before producing his first novel, "Phyllis in Bohemia," in 1898 to tepid reviews. Barbour switched to sports fiction with "The Halfback" the following year and changed his career for good.

The story follows young Joel March from an uncertain Maine farm boy to an athletic and social success as a Harvard freshman, and was an enormous success. Barbour's accounts of sporting events were unlike any others presented to young readers at the time. They were exciting, lively and close-up, putting the reader directly in the midst of the game and capturing the intensity and verve of young men fully involved in sports. Barbour provided an immediacy that was lacking from other writers of this period.

AGAIN THE CHAP WITH THE GREAT GREEN S DECORATING his jersey went through his contortions, and the sphere sped forward. Gray struck at it with all his force and spun around on his heel. The catcher dropped to his knee and picked the ball from the dust. It was a most deceptive drop and the waiting batsmen on the bench nodded their heads in approval.

"Two strikes!"

A little spot of deeper red shone on Gray's cheek now and he moved his

stick a bit nervously behind his shoulder. The pitcher stepped back into his box, nodded to a sign from the catcher, and let drive. Then there was a sharp report as Gray's bat struck the speeding sphere, the grand stand was on its feet, the three men on bases raced home almost in a bunch, and Gray was rounding first base at a desperate pace!

High and far sped the ball. The left-fielder was racing back down the field. Would he catch it? Pandemonium reigned in the grand stand. Wayne and the others were on their feet, shouting wildly and waving their caps. Gray reached second base, cast a glance toward left field, and came on. The fielder turned almost under the ball and reached upward, leaped back a step, clutched wildly, and fell. The ball, tipping his fingers just beyond his reach, dropped to earth. And Gray, panting and happy, crossed the home plate into the arms of his exultant friends.

FOR THE HONOR OF THE SCHOOL (1900)

Over the next forty years Barbour churned out nearly 150 more volumes ranging from sports fiction to stories for young girls (it was assumed that only boys would be interested in reading about sports) to non-fiction works. My favorite title in his ouevre was a 1926 travel guide, "Let's Go to Florida," succinctly subtitled "Information For Those Who Haven't Been But Are Going, Those Who Have Been and Are Going Back, and Those Who Don't Expect to Go But Will."

Barbour's skill evidently enabled him to produce books virtually upon demand and were quickly considered best sellers in the limited world of juvenile fiction, and his prolific quantity provided him with a comfortable existence, three wives, and a slightly guilty exuberance that he was being paid to do what he liked best.

"Most of [my books] are for the younger generation," he wrote in 1934, "since, having accustomed myself to viewing life from the juvenile point, I find it difficult to see it from the grown-up's angle." He died in Pass Christian, Mississippi, in 1944, having spanned the period from genteel amateur athletics through the Golden Age to a period of uncertainty.

AND THEN THERE WAS THE BOWDITCH GAME! Arnold quailed when he thought of that test. Of course he would make a failure of it. Bill Regan expected him to, even seemed to want it. He marveled at the pleasure with which he had received that announcement. Now he would be quite as well pleased if Billy hadn't made such a foolish promise. For of course it was foolish. Bowditch was a big school, with a big squad of ball players. Bowditch would probably hammer even Clayt McKenzie to all points of the compass, so what chance had Arnold Chase? None at all, thank you! Maybe it would be just as well if he became seized by a sudden and mysterious malady before Saturday!

THE RELIEF PITCHER (1927)

Barbour's fiction was different from what had come before. He portrayed real boys with real faults playing real games — admittedly in somewhat unreal settings — using descriptions unequalled during his period. Barbour wrote dramatically of contests in all sports, including such unlikely ones as golf, rowing and track. His work was decidedly formulaic and episodic; hence he was a prime candidate for repeated (and lucrative) serialization in juvenile magazines like St. Nicholas.

MARCH CAME BLUSTERING IN WITH CLOUDY skies and cold winds. But in a week it had changed its tune. One morning Dan awoke to find the sunlight streaming through the front windows and a new quality in the air. For a moment he lay under the covers and wondered sleepily what it was that brought the strange stirring to his heart. Then he was out of bed, had thrown the window wide open, and was leaning forth in his pajamas breathing in the warm, moist air. Spring had come in the night. All about him were signs. Above was a mellow blue sky dotted with little feathery white clouds. In the roadway beneath the snow was melting fast and the gutters were astream with trickling water. Even the stone window coping under his hands seemed somehow to hint of Spring; it was warm to his fingers and moist where a little rim of ice had melted. There was a faint, heart-cheering aroma of brown earth and greening sod released from their winter coverings. Dan gave a shout and drew his head in long enough to awaken Gerald.

"Get up!" he cried. "It's Spring, Gerald! Get up and hear the birdies sing!"

DOUBLE PLAY (1909)

The heart of Barbour's works lay in their setting: the boys' private school of the privileged. Fictionalized accounts of a boy's paradise — plenty of sports and hijinks, and a minimum of studying — produce a picture of an elite life more suited to colleges, complete with little adult supervision, comfortable dorm rooms and the indolent lifestyle of old money. Barbour was frequently asked by wistful readers as to the whereabouts of such havens as Yardley, Ferry Hill and Hillton and was forced to admit that they did not exist, save through his pen. Significantly it was not until his final books that Barbour changed his settings to public high schools, with little appreciable difference in plot or characterization. Compare the Barbour settings with those of his most notable juvenile successor, John R. Tunis, who found his voice effectively through the democracy of the public high school, and effectively contrasts it with the private academy in "All-American."

Barbour's "townies" are usually poor or working class, ethnically stereotypical (Jews are crafty, Irish good-hearted tipplers) and often-times deferential to the young gentlemen at school. Only Barbour would make a millionaire's son (aptly named Gerald Pennimore) a sympathetic character in his series of Yardley School books. Boys from modest circumstances are often Barbour's heroes; but upon entering a Barbour school are usually steered toward the life of privilege after contact with their wealthier and socially adept chums. Joel Marsh in "The Halfback" is promised a law partnership while still a freshman in college based upon his pluck and skill in athletics.

THE VISITORS WERE A TOUGH-MUSCLED GANG of country-bred youths whose ages ranged from presumably thirteen to twenty. Several were elongated and weedy looking, one was surprisingly fat — he played third base and got away with it very creditably — and others were small and freckled and as full of ginger as a Canton jar. With them came a cheering section that was largely composed of shrill-voiced, wildly enthusiastic and extremely patriotic girls. Not relying entirely on the power of the human lungs, quite a few had brought bicycle or automobile horns. Many of the home-team players hated these horns intensely before the game was over.
THE RELIEF PITCHER (1927)

Barbour's value today is more than an outdated look at class and education in early 20th century America. His knowledge of sports and ability to translate it to exciting prose made him unique among authors at that time. Robert Cantwell in Sports Illustrated observes that Barbour created more interesting and exciting fictional games than actual contests as they were being reported in contemporary newspapers of the time, and suggests that Barbour's success increased the quality of sports reporting from others who now had higher standards to reach with young readers.

...THE HEAD COACH NODDED.

"I was wondering," he said dryly, "how long it would take you fellows to find that out. I might have told you about it after the first inning, but I thought I'd just wait and see how much baseball sense you all had. So far, Loring, you appear to be the only one with enough gumption to study the situation." Durfee blinked and colored. Payson turned to him quizzically. "Durfee, couldn't you have made that discovery just as well as Loring? Seems to me it would have come better from you, as captain. But the trouble was you lost your temper just as soon as you found you couldn't hit Holmes, and instead of looking around to see where the trouble lay you just went up there and hit out blindly at anything he offered you. Isn't that about the way of it?"

"I guess so," acknowledged the captain, looking not a little chagrined.

FOR YARDLEY (1911)

Barbour's fictional characters soon became a central theme to his books, more so than who won the game. Seldom are his figures influenced by adults, save for the occasional coach. They live by themselves, solve their own problems, and grow or diminish through their own efforts. It is difficult to remember that Barbour's boys are sixteen or seventeen, for they appear much older. There is no difference between his few college stories and his prep school tales.

However, Barbour was not without an acute knowledge of the exuberance and poignancy of youth. Time spent at school was fleeting, and his characters frequently reflect on the passing of time and the

uniqueness of this period of life. While the characters would move on to college and success, Barbour would remain back at school recycling his tales for a new set of characters and readers.

ONE MORNING IN LATE MARCH THE EARTH *awoke to find that during the night a little south wind had melted the last vestige of ice and snow in the shaded corners, and that Spring was busy cleansing the land ere beginning her housekeeping. The gravel walks were soft underfoot and little blue ribbons of water trickled across them. The willows in the meadow at the base of the hill had suddenly put on their vernal costume of tender russet, and the campus, a veritable quagmire for the nonce, was doffing its faded livery, and, to the close observer, revealing in favored hollows and sheltered slopes a garb of soft green velvet. Along the station road the thrush proclaimed its pleasure at the new order of things in clear, sweet notes that trembled in the soft air like intangible sunflecks. The river rehearsed in gentle murmurs a new song as it rippled past island and point, and reflected on its bright surface the tender blue of the sky and the fleecy whiteness of the slowly sailing clouds. Spring had come in the valley of the Hudson.*

And never was spring more welcome. The winter had been severe and protracted, and to youth and health the enforced captivity indoors had long since grown irksome.Suddenly the boathouse became the scene of much activity and the two crews took to the water with all the delight of young ducks, and the sound of oars and of the coxswains' voices floated up from the river every afternoon. Baseballs and bats made their appearance and swept through the school like an epidemic. The campus became the center of Academy life, and the gold links was [sic] dotted with enthusiastic players.

FOR THE HONOR OF THE SCHOOL (1900)

Barbour's baseball stories are usually part of a cyclical book that follows its boys through a school year or term. The spring and baseball season come as a release from the confinements of winter. As we celebrate baseball as an expression of yearly renewal and pastoral innocence, it is interesting to observe that Barbour wrote of the same feelings nearly a century ago.

WINTER PASSED AT LAST. THE SOUTHERN hillsides lay bare of snow and tiny watercourses appeared in unsuspected places. Spring made her appearance hesitantly, even bashfully, but having arrived she remained, becoming more certain in her role each day. Green spaces magically appeared in the meadows, willows awakened and the first robin, official harbinger of spring, was reported from dozens of widely separated places. What a busy bird he is, to be sure, and how he must hurry and bustle to cover his huge territory on time! Sometimes one wonders if there aren't two of him.

Fortunate are those whose playing fields, like that at Channery School, are on the hills and have a natural slope. The diamond was dry enough for practice a week before the lowland meadows ceased squishing underfoot, and on an afternoon not far from the middle of the month Coach Regan led his charges outdoors. There had been a fortnight of work in the cage in the basement of the gymnasium, and now this was a vast relief. They look to the fields like colts to the pasture, and even Augustus Abraham Anderson sang to himself as he pushed his wheelbarrow across the yielding turf. Gus was colored and middle-aged, and he served as rubber, grounds keeper - with the assistance of another and younger gentleman of his race - and janitor of the gymnasium building. His official title, bestowed by himself, was Assistant Trainer. He had been at Channery so long that, had precedence been determined solely by length of service, he would have mounted the platform at Commencement ahead of Doctor Cavanaugh.

THE RELIEF PITCHER (1927)

Ralph Henry Barbour certainly had his faults as a writer. His plots are often unimaginative, his writing differs little from one book to the next, and he wrote unceasingly about a narrow section of society. But Barbour did understand the universality of sport to all boys, and retained enough youthful feelings in him to create books that appealed to his loyal readers. For two generations Barbour actively produced readable books which celebrated growing up and finding oneself through the lessons learned in baseball that encouraged children to participate in the sport. In an appreciation of baseball literature, the work of Ralph Henry Barbour should not be neglected, for he created the first modern juvenile sports fiction with lasting impact.

AND THEN THE GOAL WAS IN SIGHT and the enemy's tail-enders were up, and Arnold went out sturdily enough to hold the victory. But something was wrong now. One ball and another sped by the batter. Then a strike, doubtful but allowed by the umpire. Then a third ball. Walters walked down and said quietly; "Don't lose him, Spook. Put 'em right in the glove. Let him hit it if he can." And Arnold tried so hard with the next one, and could have wept when the umpire waved the man to first!

He tried to catch him there once, but he almost overthrew the bag and turned his attention to Pitcher Breeze. Breeze was no more of a hitter than Arnold himself, and Arnold got him out of the way with five deliveries. That strike-out gave him back some of his waning courage. The head of the Parkman list took the second delivery and sped it across the diamond, but Copp got in front of it, knocked it down, found it and sped it to Meigs in the nick of time. Two out now! The Channery stand was cheering incessantly. Arnold found himself trembling, but there was no weakness in it. It was, perhaps, rather the manifestation of a sort of joyful certainty of victory. It didn't affect his arm as he sped the ball forward, nor his eye as he followed its flight. He got one strike on a fast, straight delivery over the very center, tried a curve that failed, found the plate once more with a drop that made the formidable Gage swing wildly, sent in a high one that was too close and then risked all on another drop. Gage smiled in superior fashion as he let it go by. Bert held the ball in his hand and dashed his mask off. The umpire said "Out!" Gage gasped incredulously, would have argued, perhaps, but who with?

THE RELIEF PITCHER (1927)

PHILIP BERGEN is librarian for the Bostonian Society.

'Why Not Let Ruth Hit?'

By William Curran

WHEN AS A BOY I eavesdropped on the conversations of adult baseball fans, I scarcely ever knew my elders to be in unanimous agreement on anything. There was one notable exception: the conviction that the Boston Red Sox's pre-World War I outfield of Tris Speaker, Harry Hooper, and George "Duffy" Lewis was the greatest fielding combination ever assembled.

I knew a bit about Speaker, of course. He was a superstar from the past in a category with Cobb, Ruth and Wagner. On the other hand, Hooper and Lewis had fast become shadowy figures for most young fans. In retrospect, it is possible that I had deferentially accepted as an article of faith the older generation's judgment on the Red Sox outfield of 1910-1915. But I doubt

---

HARRY HOOPER:
An American Baseball Life
by Paul J. Zingg
University of Illinois Press, 1993, 281
pp., $27.50

---

it, especially since I had already seen in action an outfield like Pittsburgh's Paul and Lloyd Waner and Fred Lindstrom and would soon be admiring Yankees Joe DiMaggio, Tommy Henrich and Charley Keller and Cardinals Stan Musial, Terry Moore and Enos Slaughter. In any case, Harry Hooper's name stuck in my mind as one whose play had once been held in high regard.

In 1971, forty-six years after Hooper closed out his major league career he was named by the Veterans Selection Committee to the Baseball Hall of Fame in what Bill James, among others, has characterized as an idiosyncratic choice. James does not rank Hooper among the top 100 ballplayers for either Peak Value or Career Value. John Thorn, Pete Palmer, Donald Honig and Lawrence Ritter concur.

I am not qualified to judge

whether or not Hooper belongs in Cooperstown. The record of Hooper's 17-year career in the American League suggests to me what fifty years ago they used to call a "solid" ballplayer: talented, dependable, consistent in performance but a cut below superstar rank. As a matter of fact, I rarely hear that succinct assessment of a ballplayer these days, although there are still players in the majors who deserve the label. Terry Pendleton of the Atlanta Braves, Robby Thompson of the Giants, Mark Grace of the Cubs, Brett Butler of the Dodgers, Terry Steinbach of the Athletics and perhaps a couple of dozen more.

One clear mark of Harry Hooper's solidity was that in the sixteen seasons after he became a Red Sox regular in 1910, he played an average of 139 games. Surely in those years, Hooper suffered injuries and illnesses, suffered batting slumps, faced family problems and dealt with miscellaneous lesser distractions. And there were the war years with their abbreviated schedules and other disruptions. Apparently, on most days during that decade and a half, Harry Hooper pulled on his spikes and was ready for duty.

Author Paul Zingg, professor of history at St. Mary's College of Moraga, California, who also serves as Dean of the School of Liberal Arts, offers several reasons for deciding to undertake a comprehensive and scholarly study of the

baseball career of a figure like Harry Hooper. First there was the fact that Hooper was a St. Mary's alumnus. Curiously, Dean Zingg, a longtime Red Sox fan, was already established at the college before he first learned this. In any case, the dean's earlier inclination to do a study of baseball as it related to American society now shifted to take the form of a biography of Hooper as a representative professional ballplayer of the first quarter of the century.

"More Everyman than Superman," Dean Zingg writes, "he [Hooper] is a mirror of the game and its human touches in ways that his myth-encrusted contemporaries can never be."

Once Dean Zingg had examined Hooper's major league record closely, he concluded that Harry had been a better ballplayer than today's number-crunching baseball analysts are ready to acknowledge, noting for example that Hooper still holds some all-time fielding records.

In Dean Zingg's view there were a number of things that made Hooper a potentially rewarding subject for study by an American historian. Hooper was the son of immigrants. He had grown up in rural, mostly agrarian, circumstances. Harry, along with Christy Mathewson, Eddie Collins, Eddie Plank, Jack Barry and others was also among the first substantial group of

college-educated players to enter professional baseball. Finally, Hooper was a Californian, part of the earliest wave of major league players from a state that would prove the most fertile source of baseball talent for this century.

Harry Hooper was born in 1887 in the sparsely populated and still beautiful Santa Clara Valley of California. Despite the tendency of his restless father Joe Hooper to move from homestead to homestead in the valley, Harry always looked back on his country boyhood in California as idyllic. The youngest of four Hooper children, Harry was not only strong and athletic but also excelled in the classroom. When he was about fifteen, one of Harry's teachers urged Joe and Mary Hooper to let their son continue his education as far as his abilities would carry him. Although finan cially hard pressed, the Hoopers, like so many immigrant parents of the period, were prepared to strain family resources to see that at least one of their children, in this case the youngest, should have the opportunity to improve his situation. And so they enrolled young Harry in the secondary school attached to St. Mary's College.

Harry put this parental sacrifice to good account. Six years later he had earned his degree in Civil Engineering and accepted a job with the Southern Pacific Railroad, a position that seemed to offer a secure and perhaps prosperous future. But the young engineer was also an athlete; and this is where his story becomes a characteristically American one. Harry had had the good fortune to play in his senior year on what Dean Zingg describes as "arguably one of the greatest nines in the history of the collegiate game," St. Mary's 1907 champions, called the Phoenix, who won 27 games and lost none. The 1907 Phoenix would send no fewer than six men into the professional ranks.

With a league-leading .371 batting average, Phoenix leftfielder Hooper attracted his share of attention from professional scouts, and as a consequence in 1908 the ex-collegian found himself juggling the duties of a surveyor for the railroad and an outfielder for the Sacramento Sacts of the Pacific Coast League. So well did Hooper perform in his part-time stint on the ball field that by 1909 he was on the way to join the Boston Red Sox at a rookie salary that considerably exceeded what he earned from the railroad. It is interesting to note that as much as major-league ballplayers had complained over the decades about being underpaid — and that was almost certainly true in light of their talent — baseball salaries apparently topped beginning pay in the learned professions.

In his dozen years with Boston, Hooper became one of the Ameri-

can League's most respected leadoff batters and a fielder without peer. Dean Zingg suggests that Hooper's qualities as a field leader on teams that included stars like Tris Speaker, Smoky Joe Wood, Hugh Bedient, Babe Ruth, Larry Gardner, Duffy Lewis, and Bill Carrigan account in large measure for the high regard in which he was held by players, fans and the press. In the space of six seasons, Hooper helped lead the Sox to four world championships. In time, he was named Boston's team captain.

One instance of the leadership Hooper exercised with the Red Sox has taken on the aura of legend. In the wartime season of 1918, with the Red Sox strapped for hitting, team captain Hooper persuaded new manager Ed Barrow to play lefthanded pitching ace Babe Ruth in the outfield or at first base between starts. Hooper had already calculated the value of Babe's booming bat. When the war ended Hooper argued for playing Babe full time in the outfield — and got his way. The consequences for Ruth and for the history of baseball were revolutionary.

In the deliberate breakup of the great Red Sox organization following World War I, Hooper was traded to the Chicago White Sox in 1921. After turning in five steady seasons of play for Chicago, Harry retired in 1925. For a brief period in the 1930s, he was baseball coach at Princeton, but fell victim to Depression budget cuts. In 1932 Harry returned to his hometown of Capitola, California, where he found a comfortable life, working as a real estate agent and serving for almost 25 years as local postmaster. He died in 1974 at the age of 87.

In doing research for the book, Dean Zingg had the singular good fortune to unearth several diaries that Hooper had kept when he first went to the majors. These day-by-day accounts offered invaluable insights from an intelligent and educated observer into the life of a professional player in the years before World War I.

"Harry Hooper: An American Baseball Life" is a sound and richly annotated study not only of Hooper's life and baseball career but of the times in which he played. Not the least virtue of Dean Zingg's book is that it is very well written, in a graceful, easy prose that is pleasant to read.

The University of Illinois Press must be commended for supporting studies like Dean Zingg's, which not only enlarge the canon of sports history but also bring significant aspects in our national life into sharper focus.

BILL CURRAN is the author of "Mitts: A Celebration of Fielding" and "Big Sticks: The Batting Revolution of the 1920s and '30s."

The Seasons in the Attic

by Gene Carney

BEFORE AGREEING TO review Wilfrid Sheed's "My Life As a Fan," I confessed a prejudice in his favor — I've been a Sheed fan for a long time. After, I confess a second prejudice, which makes me hope that his book succeeds wildly, generating many more like it: I'm very biased toward fans' books, and Sheed's memoir is precisely that. By a fan, about fans, for fans.

Sheed's literary swing through his "attic" of fandom (where dusty memories rest, until stirred by visitors, when they take on vivid colors and bubble like a fountain of youth) is compact, but touches all the important bases. It can be enjoyed on your own level of intensity: as a Brooklyn Dodger fan still buoyed by the forties and fifties, and still furious enough to organize a lynching, should Walter O'Malley

ever appear near "his roots"; and by all baseball fans, who will be sent climbing into their own attics, for parallel and echoed remembrances.

Novices in any religious organization are separated from those who practice only occasionally, by a head to toe plunge into a spiralling liturgical year, where faith is front-and-center daily, while the rest of the world settles for the second division. "My Life" is Sheed's recollection of his own formative years in the religion of baseball — three-quarters of the book focus on the seasons between 1940 and 1945, when he aged from 9 to 14. His stories from later years are worth the telling, but his best stuff is spent in these early innings.

Yet finally, how blithely we all of us made these lifelong commitments. One guy would make his vows because a

---

MY LIFE AS A FAN
By Wilfrid Sheed
Simon and Schuster, 1993.
224 pp., $20

favorite teacher liked the Giants; another would bind himself over for life because there were more Italians on the Yankees right now. Becoming a Dodger fan in 1941 seems, in retrospect, like signing on for the Confederate army or the losing side in the Thirty Years War. You march into the recruiting office with a spring in your step and a song in your heart, expecting the glory to begin immediately. But then, there is a slight delay.

Sheed's path to this nation's peculiar brand of inter-urban warfare began with a reading phase, as a youngster from England whose family sought shelter from the Nazi storm in 1940 Philadelphia. Photos and stories in The Saturday Evening Post and Life delivered the hook. Phase two was playing the game; Phase three, radio (Red Barber reeled him in.)

Many fans can talk forever about their "first fields," those neighborhood games on scrub grass or concrete, when the rules were still not quite memorized, and who kept score? Radio games, of course, can *still* be better than being there, the imagination tickled in ways that television (almost a villain today, its capacity to change the sport, not necessarily for the better, aside) never can.

There are treats for readers in Sheed's sketches of Mack, Durocher, Rickey, Ruth ("clown or no clown, he was deadly serious about this one thing, and played the game quite flawlessly, which means with total concentration"), and his own heroes, Pistol Pete Reiser and Brooklyn's boys of the wartime summers.

His album is likewise filled with mental photos that nicely chronicle the day's pennant chases and World Series, all snapped from vantage points familiar to fans — the lines are only crossed briefly to snatch an autograph here and there, four in all.

Sheed's penlight bounces off the ballroom mirror-globe of fans' feelings, scattering them so they illuminate the pages. Not just the common varieties of rooting, either, although that would have been plenty. No, Sheed also captures the symptoms of withdrawal that winters cause; the competition for hearts between baseball and football, or, in his case, cricket (he's back in England by 1946, his private war with polio and the world's with Hitler over); the irony of the triumph of lesser teams; the hatred of rivals and of Yankees; and finally, the rewards of seeing the game with "fresh eyes," of rediscovering an old friend after being out of touch. "Such is the sweep of base-

ball history that it picks up for you in your absence and fills you in upon your return like a chatty landlady who is always bursting with news for you."

The book is not flawless — neither was Ruth. But I forgave each overuse of the adjective "goofy" because there were so many more terrific lines and paragraphs. For example, "This is the price you pay for playing teams like the Red Sox and the old Dodgers. You will beat them, of course, but the only games you will ever hear about afterwards are the ones in which *they* did something." Exhibit A could be the '47 Series — Sheed viewed the hit off Bevens by Lavagetto, the only one the Bums needed that day, on a TV behind a crowded bar, an underage teen nursing a ginger ale. I saw Fisk's homer in '75 from the same angle, without any sound but the pandemonium of patrons. Exhibit B.

Sheed notes his father's "weakness for sports" but I wish he'd have elaborated some here: the genetic factor in fandom is still one of the least examined, I think, beyond those backyard games of catch with dad.

"My Life as a Fan" is a refreshing break from the present, though Sheed writes it, finally, as a '90s Mets fan. It's no retreat into a schmaltzy yesteryear, however, even though it's a visit to seasons of infatuation, and is heavy with nostalgia. (There's Newk, punching out a parking attendant after Game 7 in '56, but that was understandable and forgivable, no? — unlike O'Malley's move west a year or so later.)

Readers need not like their baseball served up ala Roger Angell or George Will to enjoy "My Life as a Fan." But that will help. Yankee fans are advised to wear some armor. For all others, slippers and a comfortable chair will do it.

GENE "TWO FINGER" CARNEY is the author of "Romancing the Horsehide: Baseball Poems on Players and the Game" (McFarland & Co.). He edits the fans' newsletter "Notes from the Shadows of Cooperstown" as a hobby from his home base in Utica.

How Good Were They?

By Mat Olkin

Y EARS AGO, WHEN BILL James first started writing his annual Baseball Abstracts, he was told that there was no market for such a book. Conventional "wisdom" held that the public possessed neither the patience nor the intelligence to follow James' complex technical analysis. By voraciously consuming the Abstract, however, the "public" was making a statement. We are smarter than you think, we said. We passed algebra in high school, and we like to think we have a little common sense, and so we are not, in fact, wholly unequipped to grapple with something as "technical" as Sabermetrics. Oh — and by the way, we appreciate not being presumed to be idiots.

This lesson was lost on John P. McCarthy, Jr. Although his attempt to select the all-time all-star team is soundly reasoned, he depreciates his otherwise intriguing analyses by consistently underestimating the reader. He assumes that we still can't grasp Sabermetrics, so he contrives his own numbers, which are, by comparison, simplistic rather than simple. When he summarizes the highlights of Willie Mays' career, he thinks we still need to be filled in about the Vic Wertz episode.

Nonetheless, the book's overall concept and approach are commendable. In selecting the all-time bests at each position, his analysis is thorough and usually well-reasoned. First, he attempts to measure objectively each player's contributions at the plate and in the field. Next, McCarthy takes the important step of incorporating the opinions of writers, players, and coaches. His stated goal is, "to respect both fact

---

BASEBALL'S ALL-TIME DREAM TEAM
By John P. McCarthy, Jr.
Betterway Books, 1994, 232 pp.,
$12.95

and fancy, and search for the appropriate balance between statistics and opinions." Each player's final ranking combines his offensive and defensive ranking, together with the historical consensus as to the player's place in history. Thus, his resulting selections are supported — to varying degrees — by both the consensus of authority and the weight of the evidence.

First, let me tell you about the author's biases. John P. McCarthy, Jr. grew up in New York in the '50s, so it is not surprising to find that he has a sentimental weakness for home runs in general and Mickey Mantle in particular. To his credit, he did realize that Sabermetrics was the best tool for evaluating players' performances across different eras. He admittedly finds Sabermetrics to be overly technical, and certainly he is not alone. However, when he assumes that his readers share this view, and that therefore he must simplify everything for them, he drops the ball.

Now, let me tell you about my biases. I consider myself a Sabermetrician, so when I see sloppy work it really peeves me (McCarthy's use of flawed methods gets under my skin, but if you don't pay attention to that type of stuff, just disregard all my carping). Besides that, I can't agree with anyone who says that Sabermetrics is beyond the ken of the average fan. You don't need to have an understanding of regression analysis, a scientific calculator, or (even) geeky glasses in order to understand Sabermetrics; all you really need are two things that most of us already possess: a basic understanding of (1) math, and (2) the game of baseball. Sabermetrics is not quantum physics, and if it were, the Abstract would never have become the best-selling annual baseball book. But we, the public, have been underestimated many times before.

In the past decade, Sabermetrics has made its way into the discussion of many "mainstream" baseball concerns. Sabermetric methods have been employed in the ongoing and timeless argument about the greatest players at each position, and about how the oldtimers stack up against today's heroes. The two manifestos on the subject were John Thorn and Pete Palmer's "The Hidden Game of Baseball" and Bill James' "Historical Baseball Abstract." By rigorously employing state-of-the-art Sabermetrics, these two books set the standard for all books to come.

McCarthy does not attempt to improve upon those two seminal works. He merely seeks to borrow their approaches in measuring players' offensive and defensive contributions. The problems come when McCarthy, working on the assumption that this earlier work was too

inaccessible for the average fan, attempts to simplify matters. As a result, his method for measuring offensive production contains obvious errors, and fails to yield the simplicity he presumes our feeble minds require.

Sabermetricians in particular will take issue with McCarthy's "Ultimate Batting Statistic": his "Earned Bases Average" ("EBA"). As a tool for measuring offense, the formula is no great step forward: it is conspicuously similar to other formulas such as Thomas Boswell's Total Average, trudging down the well-worn path of estimating a player's bases gained per out made. For his "stat" to have any credibility, it must correlate with runs scored — James' Runs Created does, as does Palmer's Linear Weights. In other words, to show that EBA accurately measures offensive production, McCarthy must show that teams with the highest EBAs score the most runs. But the author makes no attempt to verify this; he simply assumes that his stat measures offense, and proceeds on that assumption. "My EBA," he blankly asserts, "works well... and is the best single statistic for the job." We are expected to take this on faith.

In fact, McCarthy takes it upon himself to challenge one of the most fundamental axioms of Sabermetrics: the idea that the batter's job is to create runs for his team. Offense is the scoring of runs, by definition. McCarthy, however, seems to think that the batter's job is to merely accumulate bases, with any resulting runs the team may score coming as a purely incidental benefit. In sum, while McCarthy's EBA purports to measure offense, it actually measures bases, a related but distinctly separate category. Later, in adjusting the numbers for park effects, McCarthy makes other technical mistakes which hardly deserve elaboration. Suffice to say that he elevates Babe Ruth and Bill Dickey because their stats were supposedly "hurt" from playing in Yankee Stadium. If you are reading this we can already assume that you know better. While the asymmetrical Stadium was tough on right-handed hitters, for lefties, it was hardly "The House That Waite Hoyt Built."

Even more annoying are his swipes at some of the more legitimate work which has been done in the area of offensive measurement. First, he goes after Bill James himself, disparaging the Runs Created formula for expressing production in terms of runs rather than bases. Converting earned bases into estimated runs, says McCarthy, is, "an unnecessary step...(which) just complicates the matter." Again, if you recognize that the purpose of an offense is to score runs, you may beg to differ. Next, he snubs Thorn

and Palmer's commonly used "PRO" stat (on-base average plus slugging percentage). McCarthy claims "(it) has no inherent meaning, and is just another contrived number." Perhaps he's right, but if he is, what makes his EBA any less contrived?

It quickly becomes apparent that McCarthy has a sentimental bias toward the home run that has no place in an objective study of offense. He mentions Palmer's Linear Weights system for analyzing offense, but ultimately rejects it, claiming that Palmer undervalued the home run. Fair enough; Palmer's system is meticulously calculated and widely accepted, but if McCarthy can claim that he's improved on it, any good Sabermetrician would love to see his evidence. He has none. McCarthy weights the homers more heavily simply because he likes them — and I'm not kidding. He sounds much more like Bart Giamatti than Bill James when he celebrates "the transcendent beauty to great hits," and goes on to "challenge a mathematical construct which devalues the extra bases earned by sluggers." It's no wonder that his EBA stat unduly favors sluggers, and sometimes yields absurd results, such as ranking Darryl Strawberry as the eighteenth-best hitter of all time. However, it should be said in all fairness that the EBA is so similar to other proven performance measures that it probably does retain some significance.

It is in his analysis of defensive statistics where McCarthy achieves his desired combination of accuracy and simplicity. He uses players' conventional fielding stats and compares them to the league averages for the relevant era. The results are surprisingly consistent with the prevailing opinions, and give new insight into players' fielding abilities, especially the early-century stars. For example, it is interesting to see who got to more balls (relative to the league) — Tris Speaker or Willie Mays. I never got to see Roberto Clemente play, but after looking at his numbers, it is obvious that his throwing arm's legendary reputation is entirely justified. Still, McCarthy properly recognizes the limitations of the meager defensive stats, and accordingly gives greater weight to the opinions when calculating his defensive rankings.

If there is one reason to buy this book, it is Chapter Four: "The Opinions." McCarthy exhaustively surveys the authoritative opinions, striving to find a consensus pick at each position. Surveys of the players and writers are included; we even get the cumulative MVP ballots cast for each player. McCarthy incorporates the contemporary opinions of participants like Connie Mack, Ty Cobb, and Walter Johnson. To lend a dose of

detached objectivity, McCarthy considers the Sabermetric rankings of Thorn, Palmer and James.

It is surprisingly seldom that a true consensus emerges, underlining the fact that these debates are still very much alive. Another intriguing aspect is seeing how opinions about players change over time. For example, Rogers Hornsby has ultimately come to be accepted as one of the top three second basemen of all time. However, his contemporaries' opinions of him were, shall we say, not nearly as flattering. McCarthy places great weight on the opinions of contemporaries, and with good reason. Great hitting, he reminds us, is tabulated for posterity, while great fielding inevitably fades from memory.

McCarthy is also able to revitalize the stardom of players who have long since faded from the common memory. He shows us that Buck Ewing, in his day, was regarded as perhaps the best player of them all. Such recognition cannot be lightly dismissed, and McCarthy rightfully honors Ewing along with Bench and Berra. In sum, this chapter is one of the most exhaustive and valuable surveys of historical opinion on the subject.

The rest of the book is just empty calories. In the "Up Close And Personal" section, we get a short profile for each member of McCarthy's "team." Typically, the profile runs a page and a half and adds nothing to the knowledge of an informed reader. Not surprising, considering that McCarthy feels compelled to include glossary definitions for things like "hits," "ERA," and "RBI." At times, I even wondered if McCarthy's refusal to address a more sophisticated audience stemmed from a lack of *capability* rather than a lack of will: he refers to Pete Alexander's "legendary strikeout of Tony Lazzeri in the 1950 World Series," and later tells us that Lou Gehrig "played in a record 2039 straight games." These are small errors, admittedly, but they can hardly give us faith in the author's knowledge of the game.

All in all, a mixed bag. If you hold an interest in this topic, McCarthy does move the discussion a small bit forward, but the subject matter must hold your attention, because the direct and ordinary writing will not. While some sections can be original and intriguing, your enjoyment of this book, unfortunately, will vary inversely with your level of knowledge.

MAT OLKIN is a regular contributor to the fantasy baseball newsletter "The Fantasy Oberver," and was a contributing editor for the 1994 edition of Paul Seibel's annual "Absolutely Baseball." He is currently creating a database for major league baseball consultant Craig Wright.

A New Look at an Old Legend

By James S. Distelhorst

N EGRO LEAGUE BASE-ball —pre-integration African-American baseball — is now "in." It is no longer the idiosyncratic interest of boutique baseball clothing mail order businesses, such as Ebbets Field Flannels and the Cooperstown Ball Cap Company, or of sometime students of the baseball arcane, such as the Society for American Baseball Research (SABR), to which I belong. No, Negro League baseball is now in the mainstream, as documented by Ray Dandridge's obituary this past winter in The New York Times; by the volume of Negro League paraphernalia, especially caps, now available at your — or at least my — local generic sporting goods store; by Negro League player game cards now available for some tabletop baseball

---

DON'T LOOK BACK: SATCHEL PAIGE IN THE SHADOWS OF BASEBALL
By Mark Ribowsky
Simon and Schuster, 1994, 351 pp. (inc. index), $23

---

games; and by the almost exponential growth in the volume and variety of books published on the Negro Leagues not just this year but in the last several years, including coffee table-sized collections of photographs. I write this sitting in my office surrounded by a Negro League Homestead Grays pennant, a 1994 Negro League calendar, and various images of Satch's fellow Negro Leaguer/Hall of Famer Buck Leonard, as I wear my own reproduction 1938 Grays cap, having for the last four years coached boys' baseball teams, each called the Grays.

Yes, Negro League baseball is now, somewhat ironically, politically correct. And "Don't Look Back: Satchel Paige in the Shadows of Baseball" by Mark Ribowsky is only one of several books published this

year on Negro League topics.

An icon, perhaps *the* i con, of that period of baseball history is Leroy "Satchel" Paige, a man who combines the creative syntactical wisdom and the amazing baseball

If Satchel had not been real, someone would have had to invent him, Ribowsky correctly writes.

skills of his sometime opponent Dizzy Dean, with the overall cultural importance and impact of Babe Ruth.

However icons, for their very existence, almost require iconoclasts — sort of like baseballs requiring bats. Ribowsky's goal in this book is to de-mythologize Satchel, to show us, as the dustjacket states, "the real Satchel Paige in the context of his times." He contends that much of Satchel's life as we know it was indeed invented.

My fear in beginning this book was that Ribowsky would be destructive and mean-spirited, holding Satchel up to a standard of behavior inappropriate to the times in which he lived. While Ribowsky at times flirts with this posture, at

one point calling his life "*sociopathic*" (emphasis his), nonetheless overall his book is a worthy addition not only to our knowledge of Satchel Paige but also to our understanding of blackball — baseball in what were then called the Negro Leagues.

Ribowsky reminds us that since the integration of baseball Satchel was the seventh black in the majors, the first black pitcher in the American League, the first black pitcher to pitch in an All-Star Game, and the first black pitcher to pitch in the World Series. Paige also was the American League Rookie of the Year when he was 46 years old, give or take a few years, some would say. Although Satchel was almost surely born on July 7, 1906 as "Leroy Page," adding the "i" later on probably to distance himself further from his father, his tombstone, however, gives "?" as his birth date, and Paige's charade of being "ageless" irritates Ribowsky. Satchel accomplished all he did despite an impoverished, largely fatherless childhood, much of it spent in a reform school seemingly forgotten by his family. Ribowsky, who did an excellent job in tracking down and interviewing some of Paige's contemporaries, quotes Willie Hines to clarify the origin of "Satchel." Leroy received this nickname not from *carrying* satchels at the local railroad station, which has been the myth, but rather from try-

ing to *steal* them.

Satchel's personal history is well-situated by Ribowsky in the full context of Negro League history. At one point Ribowsky notes the "weak overall talent of black-ball" with its stars "over romanticized" and playing against "often mediocre big leaguers," and that comparing these players to contemporary white major leaguers was "sheer fantasy." Nonetheless he does point out both when Satchel's teams beat good barnstorming teams assembled by Dizzy Dean, and Dizzy's oft-quoted high opinion of Satchel, which Ribowsky nonetheless discounts as mostly marketing.

Ribowsky makes clear his lack of respect for some of Paige's behavior which Satchel himself glossed over or simply omitted in his autobiography, "Maybe I'll Pitch Forever," as did other more hagiographic biographers. These issues include recurrent marital difficulties, habitual philandering, and frequent contract jumping to that moment's most lucrative offer. Satchel's principal loyalty was always to himself.

Nevertheless "Don't Look Back," almost by counterpoint, chronicles well Paige's long term professional relationships with the maverick major leaguer owner, Bill Veeck, and the Kansas City Monarch owner, J.L. Wilkinson.

Also included are such pearls as Satch's attachment to his favorite

catcher, Bill Perkins, and the idiomatic pronunciation of the Elite Giants as the "E-light" Giants. During World War II, Ribowsky writes, Satchel was probably the "highest-paid athlete in the world," and he did set several major league ballpark attendance records.

While highlighting Paige's poorly controlled anger which surfaced with his 1971 inclusion in Cooperstown's Baseball Hall of Fame, Ribowsky fails to mention the possible impact of Ted Williams' surprising 1966 Hall of Fame induction speech on Satchel's inclusion when Ted said: "I hope some day Satchel Paige and Josh Gibson will be voted into the Hall of Fame as symbols of the great Negro players who are not here only because they weren't given the chance."

On a more technical side, Ribowsky's repeated using of the contemporary term "dissed" to mean "criticized" struck me as false. The book's 12 page index is indeed welcome and excellent.

However, although there were only several minor typos, there was one major publishing problem worthy of note: pages 80 and 81 somehow were switched. What that means is that in order to read the book continuously, as it was written, one has to read from page 79 to page 81, and then back to page 80, that followed by page 82. I am sure

this problem will be remedied in future printings.

Fellow Negro League pitcher Connie Johnson perhaps situates Paige best and most appropriately within his own culture. Satchel, he told Ribowsky,

> was like a Babe Ruth to us, but he was *our* Babe Ruth. I think it's hard for people nowadays to understand how big he was. He was like the biggest guy we knew. It didn't make no difference what kinda stuff he did, 'cause that only made him *more* bigger than life. And don't you believe Satchel didn't know he was, too [emphases his].

Clearly Ribowsky, in "Don't Look Back: Satchel Paige in the Shadows of Baseball," understands and appreciates this man's uniqueness while not accepting all of Satchel's myths or behavior. In situating Satchel's well-researched life and talent well within the history of blackball, and discounting the legend when appropriate, Ribowsky does all of us a favor, and perhaps even the great Satchel as well.

JIM DISTELHORST is a Family Physician and hospital Medical Director at Valley Medical Center in Renton, WA, just south of Seattle. To relax and get away from health care reform, Jim "does baseball." He is a member of SABR and a Mariner season ticket holder. He firmly believes that 1994 is the Mariners' year.

Cheering for the Home Team: Team Histories as Baseball Literature

By Peter C. Bjarkman

"One day I'm going to put this all in a book or a play. I'm going to be a writer like Ring Lardner or somebody - that's if things don't work out first with the Yankees, or the Cubs, or the Red Sox, or possibly the Tigers....If I get down to the St. Louis Browns, then I'll definitely be a writer." **Neil Simon, "Brighton Beach Memoirs"**

FOOTBALL LURES ITS LEGIONS OF BLOODTHIRSTY FANS WITH unrelenting violence. The pigskin game is spiced by the "corporate metaphor" of team play and individual sacrifice in the name of cohesive progress for the militaristic unit. Basketball has reached its current popularity through appeals of the larger-than-life (quite literally) celebrity and fantasy superhero. Baseball's appeal, by contrast, has always rested firmly on the drama of the hometown team. We live and die with the summertime adventures of the Dodgers, Cubs, Reds or perhaps the Tigers. The quixotic fortunes of a local ballclub, serving as alter-ego, provide us with lasting early

lessons about the ebb and flow of a life in which sobering defeat always comes hard on the heels of almost any euphoric victory.

Thus while we have carbon copy "football fans" (of both NFL and collegiate varieties) and MTV-generation basketball "hero worshippers" loyal to Air Jordan, Magic, Bird or Shaq, baseball's myriad followers come in two dozen and more species. There are Cub fans and Met fans and Yankee rooters and Tiger and Cardinal fanatics. Each inherits a colorful legacy passed down lovingly from generation to generation; each swoons summer after long summer over the ins and outs, ups and downs, pennant pursuits and endless droughts of the favored hometown team.

Baseball is simply a matter of rooting faithfully (and in most cases and for most seasons, quite hopelessly) for the cherished hometown nine. Long favored stars retire and quaint ballparks are replaced by shopping mall stadia; free agents come and go and popular performers are traded away; but it all matters very little in the long haul. Loyalty in baseball is to a logo and a uniform alone. We may grouse, groan and whine, but we seldom trade in our team for a new one.

Such loyalties are formed early in life and often have most to do with geography. They supersede and survive the ebb and flow of individual seasons as well as the comings and goings of individual star players (this is one reason why free agency and its constant player shuffling has little negative impact on the game's popularity). Part of the baggage is attachment to a particular ballpark and thus a deep connection with the events played out in that park over the course of many childhood summers. Ernie Banks will always dance gleefully in the Wrigley Field sunshine; a revamped Yankee Stadium still contains palpable ghosts of Mantle, Maris, Ruth and the Yankee Clipper. It was the loss of Ebbets Field itself, and not just the Brooklyn nameplate alone, which disenfranchised all those former Flatbush Faithful, whose own adult lives eventually took them to such distant corners of the nation. The Tigers would no longer be the Tigers without Tiger Stadium; nor would the Bosox seem legitimate anywhere but on the hallowed turf of Fenway.

It is not therefore surprising that some of baseball's finest literary works are those books which painstakingly chronicle individual team sagas. Sharing popularity with these full-fledged ballclub histories are the more episodic histories — volumes recounting certain indelible episodes (e.g., "The Boys of Summer" Dodgers) in the evolution of one historically rich ballclub or another. No set of pre-expansion-era books (with the possible exception of the Henry Wiggen novels of Mark Harris, or the ever-popular John Tunis juveniles featuring Roy Tucker of the Brooklyn Dodgers) has had more lasting appeal, for example, than the fifteen titles of the post-World-War-II Putnam team histories series penned by Fred Lieb and a handful of colleagues. Roger Kahn's classic "The Boys of Summer" owes a large part of its appeal to its status as anecdotal account of one of the most dramatic historical epochs of baseball's original "America's Team." And no genre of baseball pictorials has more takers than that devoted to the histories of particular big league clubs. For most serious and literate ball fans, in other words, reliving the baseball of our youth in print is most effectively accomplished by traveling once again that season-by-season path of a favored childhood team.

Yet if some of baseball's finest writing graces the numerous team history volumes, some of the lamest prose in the field has also been devoted to chronicling the individual team history. This writer must second Bill Carle's candid assessment (The Cooperstown Review, Volume 1) of Kip Richeal's recent opportunistic Pittsburgh Pirates history. Richeal ("The Pittsburgh Pirates: Still Walking Tall") does more to bury the proud Pirates with his penchant for cliche and syrupy prose than a half-century of rival senior circuit hurlers with their opposing fastballs. Especially exasperating, as well, is that line of team histories seizing upon a recent pennant (e.g., Rosenbaum and Stevens, "The Giants of San Francisco," 1963) or a franchise shift (Ernest Mehl, "The Kansas City Athletics," 1956) as opportunity to fuse a lame (chapter or two) superficial romp through a club's glorious or inglorious past onto a string of popular player profiles, or per-

haps an arduous game-by-game account of last fall's postseason exploits.

What then is it, precisely, that separates out the best from the rest (the Liebs and Kahns from the Richeals or Mehls) in the field of baseball team histories? My own (albeit personal) slant on the subject would suggest that the classics in this genre all share at least three obvious features. First off, the best among team histories all exploit, to greater or lesser degree, an identifiable plot structure suggesting the well-crafted novel. The truly entertaining and informative team chronicle must be one that reveals (even actively pursues) an ever-unfolding saga in the life and fortunes of a major league ballclub. The second-rate New York Highlanders first struggle in the huge shadow of McGraw's powerhouse Giants; Colonel Jake Ruppert then strikes gold by hiring manager Huggins, stealing a Babe named Ruth from Boston's lame-brained ownership and fortuitously selecting Ed Barrow as general manager; overnight a dynasty is born in "the house that Ruth built"; soon Ruth and Gehrig give way to DiMaggio and Mantle without a skipped heartbeat; "Old Professor" Stengel rewrites the book on managing; finally glory days under Topping and Webb eventually crash after a corporate takeover by the network television meddlers; the dynasty is reborn with a new set of heroes named Munson, Guidry, Martin and Jackson; enter George Steinbrenner and the villainy of the modern-ego era of baseball ownership.

This is a larger-than-life drama quite like that surrounding any truly fascinating individual or institution, and in some ways bigger in scope and more dramatic. The unremarked beauty of our national pastime is that even the lamest ballclubs seem to hold such fascination under the microscope. There is slow growth and development, rude set-back and miraculous rebound, a period of aimless wandering and an epoch of tragic near-miss. Perhaps finally a rare moment in the sun (if you're the White Sox or Phillies), and perhaps even more than one or two such moments (if you're the Yankees or Cardinals or Dodgers). The reader hopefully closes the successful team history

with a newfound indelible impression of unique franchise personality — the Cubs as hopeless but charming losers, the Yankees as the hyper-successful "company team" we all love to hate, the Blue Jays as squeaky-clean new kids on the block.

The successful baseball team history — again like the novel —is one that is also filled to the brim with lively and well-crafted actors. We have shining heroes (Mays), hopeless goats (Buckner), home-town legends (Banks) and implacable enemy warriors (like Whitey Ford, in the eyes of all Brooklyn boosters) who somehow always plague the fortunes of the favored nine, arch villains (owner Frazee of Boston) and hateful traitors (owner O'Malley in Brooklyn). Every ballclub has its full share of all these types and more. Those that have more than their alloted share hold a better likelihood of spawning a fascinating saga; these are also the very ballclubs that attract the largest fandoms — despite the mere number of pennants won or lost. Witness the Cubs and Tigers and the old Brooklyn Dodgers as our prime examples. Ernie Banks, Al Kaline, Rocky Colavito or Duke Snider do far more to inspire youthful (and thus lasting) devotion than a whole litany of pennant-winning seasons.

As a matter of course it also follows that the best-written team his-tories are those in which the author has been able to bring this cast of rich characters most fully to life, while at the same time most skill-fully plotting the ills and fortunes of a team's unfolding year-by-year and decade-by-decade saga. Any team history worth its salt is far more than a mere collection of nostalgic snapshots, or an exhaustive list of statistical flotsam (club leaders and ballclub firsts) and a com-pendium of yearly league standings.

If the best team histories feature such fully evolved plots (with the franchise itself as main character) and boast a rich cast of supporting characters in the guise of past ballclub legends, villainous and benefi-cent owners, hated goats and charming crowd-pleasers, there is also a third necessary element for the sound baseball team history. That ele-ment might best be characterized as *team personality*. Every ballclub assuredly has one, and the most interesting (and thus most passion-

ately followed) among ballclubs are those in which this visible team "character" remains largely a constant through all the upheavals of shifting eras, ownerships, stadium venues and sometimes even cities of residence. The Cubs are the nation's favorite losers, the Yankees the hated corporate bullies (even, ironically, during epochs when the New Yorkers have uncharacteristically fielded mediocre teams), the Cardinals provide a midwestern touchstone of stability, the Dodgers (during Brooklyn days to be sure) were always forthright and like-able, whether a charming set of bumbling diamond bums or glorious heroes.

As a writer of baseball team histories it has always seemed my own central task to incorporate these three elements (plot, characters, team personality) in piecing together the chronicle of any franchise. We baseball team historians are best to remember that we are pri-marily storytellers and only secondarily archivists. As a reader, it is these same three elements which I immediately search out as the true pleasure source in perusing any team history. As a critic this is also my yardstick for measuring the success of any efforts to chronicle the episodes of a ballclub's recent or lengthy past. There is, of course, another matter that is essential as well. Lively writing and proper emphasis on significant events always outweighs the accuracy of his-torical minutia. Some of my favorite team histories are also those (and there is no causal relationship here) sprinkled with the most egregious factual errors. Such is the case with the six Putnam vol-umes by Fred Lieb. Lieb occasionally slips with a date or an obscure name, especially within his Phillie and Pirate sagas. But few have ever woven a more satisfying tale, or brought more fully to life the often obscure and sometimes wooden figures of baseball's dim past. Accuracy is important, yet typos and minor bungles never mar any account of team fortunes anywhere near as much as insipid writing or the failure to bring back to life these men who ages ago created or sabotaged decades of ballclub fortunes.

The Classic Putnam Series

It is precisely the above four measures — plot, characters and team personality — all recounted in a well-focused and lively text, that obviously account for the lasting appeal enjoyed by 15 pioneering Putnam histories authored in the immediate postwar era. These books were not consistent in quality, of course, but by and large they all reached the same general level of excellence. And that excellence often came in spite of occasional historical inaccuracy or vagueness of detail.

The most interesting of the original Putnams are, of course, those that covered teams sporting the richest "Mother Lode" of colorful events and characters and touting a distinctive and appealing team personality. The Brooklyn Dodgers (1945), New York Giants (1952) and magnificent Yankees (1943), for example, are capably portrayed in tandem by New York Journal-American sports columnist Frank Graham. The pioneering first three quarters of a century of National League baseball in Cincinnati is delightfully recorded and interpreted by the immortal Lee Allen. The venerable Tigers and colorful Cardinals are brought to full life by the unsurpassed master of the first-hand-witness baseball tale, Fred Lieb. It certainly didn't hurt this entire series, of course, that fully a third of these books were indeed written by Lieb, a day-to-day journalist/historian who was also a crafty master at bringing out each of the essential elements of the successful team history formula.

The Putnam history of the Philadelphia Phillies (Fred Lieb with ex-big-leaguer Stan Baumgartner) is a particular case in point. One recent commentator bemoans Lieb's occasional historical slips. But to do so without also mentioning his immense talent at bringing to life the rare persona of the Phillie ballclub over their first half-century is to do grave injustice to one of baseball's finest books.

The Phillies were baseball's worst ballclub of the first half of the current century. Their ineptitude was matched only by their endless parade of unorthodox characters (Chuck Klein), incompetent owners (too numerous to catalogue), and circus-like playing venue (Baker

Bowl). That is to say, they were the perfect stuff of an entertaining baseball saga. No one has captured the flavor of the hapless pre-Whiz Kid Phils any better than Fred Lieb. And it is small wonder, since Lieb grew up with this very team as a boyhood fan in the waning years of the dead-ball era.

Several of Lieb's other series contributions are mini-classics as well, especially his renderings of the flamboyant Cardinals and fortune-spurned Tigers. And among the rest, Frank Graham's sagas of the Dodgers and Giants draw special merit. The first barely misses the upheaval of Robinson and Rickey (it was published in 1945) and thus focuses instead on "Daffiness Dodgers" who were anything but noble Boys of Summer. With the Giants volume, however, fortuitous timing allowed Graham to culminate his tale of glorious bygone eras (those of McGraw and Bill Terry) with the true high point of Giants history to date — the arrival of Willie Mays during the very season of Bobby Thomson's "miracle" at Coogan's Bluff.

The Putnam series of team histories is a "must read" and much-needed collectible for every serious baseball history buff. Despite the lofty fee catalogue dealers now ask for these charming books, most titles in the series can rather easily be located in big city antiquarian book shops (albeit most often without dust jackets) for prices in the neighborhood of $35 or less. It should be noted that they are not as easily acquired as a decade ago, however, and two titles — the Senators and the Phillies — are nearly impossible to locate and thus demand a premium collector's price of several hundred dollars each.

In the end, all Putnam histories to greater or lesser degree reach success by bringing out key elements of the team history formula. Warren Brown's portraits of Chicago teams are especially successful in his regard. Indeed both Chicago clubs were much closer to a dignified past when Brown completed their chronicles at the dawn of the "Golden Age" '50s. Yet Brown etches rare accounts of some of baseball's best forgotten adventures. One is the joint round-the-world exhibition tour in 1913 by Comiskey's White Sox

and McGraw's Giants, a whirlwind that climaxed with a match before the world's most staid bleacher bum, England's King George V. Then there is the account of "Trader Frank" Lane in his most successful deal, outwitting Branch Rickey to obtain the first Hispanic All-Star, flashy mid-fielder Chico Carrasquel. Also on exhibit are the "Hitless Wonders" Chicago American League club somehow stealing a 1906 pennant while sliding into history with the 90-pound-weakling team hitting average of .228.

As with all volumes of this series, the true charm of Brown's tomes is that they provide now rarely emphasized details gleaned from formative years for the national pastime, those lost seasons at the end of the 19th century and during the colorful era which spanned the nation's two world wars. Too often modern ballclub histories are filled up with the exploits of modern era stars at the expense of details about owners, managers and early ballplaying heroes who shaped ballclubs later inherited by Musial, Spahn, Mantle, Banks, Mays and Kaline.

Ballclub Pictorials and Illustrated Team Histories

As perhaps its greatest marketplace achievement the modern era of baseball books has featured glossy coffee-table volumes. Brilliant graphics, combined with new heights in production and restoration of old photographs, plus state-of-the-art color layout, have exploited the visual brilliance of the national pastime. Pictorial books have oftentimes been dismissed as second-rate literature. Yet no less a voice than Stephen Jay Gould sees them as one of baseball literature's true underappreciated treasures. In Gould's view, "picture books form the main genre for serious studies of baseball's other reality —its ability to capture an image of what we think we would like to be, if only we could shelter our world as we can confine baseball within a beautiful green diamond" (The New York Review of Books, November 1992).

Nowhere is this treasure of the nostalgic baseball image more precious than with arguably the finest team history book ever produced.

Lonnie Wheeler and John Baskin entitle their unique volume simply "The Cincinnati Game" and cover the full history of baseball's oldest and most innovative franchise from the freshest of perspectives. Perhaps the only work that comes close to anticipating Wheeler and Baskin is Louis Cauz's rare "Baseball's Back in Town: From the Don to the Blue Jays, A History of Baseball in Toronto" (Controlled Media Corporation, 1977), a fascinating study of pre-major league seasons in Canada's preeminent baseball city. The Cauz book, however, lacks a major league emphasis. And it also lacks much of the glitz and originality of the Wheeler and Baskin effort.

"The Cincinnati Game" is, foremost, a rare visual treat. And this is surprisingly accomplished without much in the way of colorful layout or glossy photography. True originality of text format is the key for Wheeler and Baskin's masterpiece. Examples of the appearance of the book simply can not be done even partial justice in mere prose description. Perhaps the centerpiece (actually laid in like a "girlie magazine" centerfold) is the striking illustration of catcher Johnny Bench ("The Annotated Bench") which proves yet again that a picture is indeed worth a thousand words and then some. Bench stands fully clothed in his "tools of ignorance" and each part of his paraphenalia is labelled with some unique career characteristic - Big Hands (mitt), Strength (chest protector), Flexibility (shin guards), Versatility (spikes) - alongside delightful accompanying explanatory text.

There are also "Timelines" that entertain and inform (greatest games; superlatives from "smallest and largest" franchise players to "worst arm and best stomach" of ballclub history; managers, executives, umpires and broadcasters; important franchise firsts, feats, facts, and fancies; legendary rhubarbs and brawls; pioneering Latins and Blacks; oddballs and clowns) that bring a unique perspective to franchise evolution. There are haunting images of both Harry Wright's pioneering 19th century Red Stockings at the dawn of the professional game and problem child Pete Rose ("Charlie Hassle" as well as "Charlie Hustle") in the twilight of the 20th century. This

book truly has to be seen and browsed to be fully appreciated. Wheeler and Baskin have set a lofty standard for all coffee table histories to follow, and few if any have so far risen to meet that challenge.

And this is a book with a rich and entertaining historical text as well. The emphasis throughout is on the arcane, the trivial, and the exotic. There is a spread on Cincinnati's numerous Spanish-speaking ballplayers; another on some surprising best and worst trades from the Reds' storied past, and one on locals who have made good (nearly 250 individuals are covered here) either with the hometown ballteam or with enemy big league clubs. But Wheeler and Baskin's appeal also lies in the fact that their very penchant for the innovative and unusual is precisely what reveals the distinctive franchise personality of the hoary Cincinnati Reds ballclub.

When it comes to pictorial team histories, however, one author alone has provided an entire industry of such books. Donald Honig — baseball's most prolific historian, if far from its best — has single-handedly produced enough picturebook histories to populate a full league or division of individual ballclubs. Honig's available titles include tomes on the New York Mets, Philadelphia Phillies, Chicago Cubs, Boston Red Sox, Brooklyn and Los Angeles Dodgers, St. Louis Cardinals and Cincinnati Reds. And more are in the works. Five of these titles have come in a spate of recent books all sharing nearly identical format. The Phillie volume is perhaps the best of this recent lot, but all have obvious weaknesses. The photographs in Honig's books are often intriguing simply because of the sheer volume of lesser-known journeyman ballplayers featured. Yet the black and white quality and layout is often unattractive, even tedious. The historical text is often rushed and does little to exploit the above-emphasized requirements of good team history writing. Only the recent Phillie book seems to bring to life anything approximating a requisite team personality.

Far better than these recent works is Honig's earlier volume on the Brooklyn Dodgers (1981). But this book also displays an identical format (a recognizable Honig formula) and thus suffers some of the

same inevitable shortcomings. Honig's books are indeed entertaining for cursory perusal. But they are hardly worth a second read (or even a first "in-depth" read) and few if any will ever stand out as classics or even valued historical contributions.

Another formulaic series of recent vintage is worth mentioning —the "Baseball's Great Dynasties" series of the early '90s produced under the label of Gallery Books (W.H. Smith Publishers). These short books are hardly in-depth histories (all are 80 pages in length), though their numerous photographs (largely drawn from the Bettman Archives) are often an unsurpassed treat. But each volume is fairly successful at some of the essentials — providing a sense of team flavor and highlighting colorful heroes and villains who mark the mileposts of each franchise history.

Some Additional Forgotten Gems

It is not possible here to survey all recent team histories, even the smaller inventory of truly exceptional titles, yet a half dozen or so books do seemingly cry out for special commentary. These are all volumes especially worthy of inclusion on any serious baseball history reading list.

One gold mine that has received surprisingly little ore extraction to date is the much-maligned and usually lackluster American League ballclub descending directly from Charlie Comiskey's infamous Black Sox outfit. Here is a franchise truly loaded with all elements of the guaranteed knockout team saga. There are strong personalities — both heroes (like Luke Appling, Minnie Minoso and Billy Pierce) and villains (Joe Jackson, Bill Veeck, and Chuck Comiskey himself). There are endless years of defeat and struggle spiced with rare but dizzying trips to the summit. There are huge heroes and hapless goats and numerous bumblers. Nothing offered by the crosstown Cubs or rival Red Sox or Tigers seems missing from the Chicago White Sox saga — except maybe in degree.

The only author to seriously tap this fertile field is Rich Lindberg. There have been a handful of other good White Sox histories, of course, especially Brown's Putnam volume already mentioned. There

is also a satisfying pictorial by Richard Whittingham (1983) which is as noteworthy for its information-packed sidebars as for its hundreds of sharp black and white visuals. But beyond that only Rich Lindberg has taken to the field — and he's done it four times.

Lindberg's best treatment of the White Sox is found in "Who's On Third?" — now more than a decade out of date (it is complete through the 1981 season). This is a book noteworthy if only for an extensive appendix of ballclub records, rosters, and minutia (trades, free agents, special rivalries like Whitey Ford versus Billy Pierce, etc.).

Lindberg's fourth volume, just released this spring, is entitled "Stealing First in a Two-Team Town." It promises to update the saga through the era of a new shopping-mall Comiskey Park and a new villainous franchise ownership under baseball's postseason revisionist, Jerry Reinsdorf. Unfortunately it was not yet available when this article was prepared.

Some team books avoid tackling the full expanse of ballclub history and instead carve out a particular era or series of episodes that make up a substantial slice of that team's overall saga. While these volumes are not by any stretch complete team chronicles, some should indeed be singled out for special mention here. Each contributes much to the history of a particular team or particular baseball-rich city.

A survey of such works might well start with Bob Buege's bittersweet account of the short-lived Milwaukee Braves. Buege's loving eulogy for a doomed sports franchise offers far more than straightforward history of the glory years for a single successful expansion team; it is also a vividly drawn portrait of the best that was baseball in those golden summers of the 1950s — before the grass was plastic, the ball parks were covered with inflatable domes, and the baseball heroes of our youth transformed into the distant media-stars and insufferable millionaire-athletes of the sound-bite electronic era.

Buege recounts the story of thirteen seasons of Brave baseball in Milwaukee (1953-1965), doing so with the rich historical detail of

the astute scholar, the gripping narrative style of the accomplished journalist, and the balanced perspective of the proficient social critic. The tale begins with a brief history of minor league baseball in Wisconsin; it details the excitement of the first arrival of Lou Perini's inept Braves from Boston in 1953; it follows season-by-season accounts of unsurpassed on-field successes in the late 1950s, and then chronicles the corporate greed and front-office bungling which only a few short seasons later would rudely transplant one of baseball's most lucrative franchises into the seemingly fertile Atlanta television market. Buege's treatment breathes life into such past diamond greats as Henry Aaron, Eddie Mathews and Warren Spahn and successfully captures the grip they once held on a single city during an all-too-brief decade which was witness to one of baseball's truly great love affairs.

T hree additional titles merit brief comment. First is Dan Turner's fascinating account of formative years for the original "Canada's Team" — Montreal's Expos. Turner's book ("The Expos Inside Out") remains to date the only book-length excuse for a legitimate history of one of baseball's most bizarre big league franchises (one that has long sported tricolor beanies instead of ballcaps, fills up its ballpark with the baseball-strange strains of the French language, and today plays its games in what appears to be a landlocked space station).

And when it comes to the offbeat and the bizarre nothing can top Charlie Finley's Athletics of the early '70s. Their saga has also been well chronicled by poet Tom Clark ("Champagne and Baloney") in a no-holds-barred account which provides both feisty history and eccentric editorial. Clark's fine-tuned portrait is of a fantastic bunch of brawlers who turned hatred of their meddling owner into the driving force of World Series victory. A final volume capturing yet another of baseball's less-glorious hours is Jack Mann's "inside story" about the destruction of the great Yankees dynasty of the Casey Stengel era ("Decline and Fall of the New York Yankees"). Mann provides convincing documentation of precisely why the unshakeable edifice built upon Babe Ruth's shoulders tumbled so quickly into

rubble in the wake of Stengel, Berra and Mantle.

Numerous other favorites might be singled out for mention. Peter Golenbock's "Bums" is the finest team book in the oral history tradition. Its limitations within the present genre are only that it covers but a single epoch, and that its organization is topical rather than chronological.

Two earlier classics about the hometown team are also especially recommended. With his fan's-eye view of the low-budget Clark Griffith ballclubs that once embarrassed the nation's capital, Morris Bealle ("The Washington Senators") proves that there is much to inspire fans even in the saga of a hopeless also-ran. James Bready provides loving detail and rare insight throughout his self-published volume entitled "The Home Team," an elegant account of the modern-day Baltimore Orioles (through the end of their "glory days" in the '60s). Bready proves an adept scholar, as well, with dense detail (including rare photos) devoted to several minor and major league forerunners that preceded the post-1950s Birds into the Chesapeake Bay city.

Finally, Dan Shaugnessy's "The Curse of the Bambino" especially displays the essential qualities of the classic team history outlined at the outset of this article. The Jekyll-and-Hyde team personality of Shaugnessey's Red Sox is indelibly drawn — here is all the horror and the heartbreak of being a true Red Sox fan. The great heroes and great villains are all here in full regalia. And the plot unfolds from tragic fatal errors marring early team history through the final denouement found in several recent decades of equally frustrating if always enchanting seasons of vain pennant pursuit.

For the would-be team historian planning to embark on his own ballclub saga, most favorite franchises (Yankees, Dodgers, Cardinals, Cubs, Tigers) today offer slim pickings. The tale of each has been well told, often several times, and only a fresh portrait with inventive theme and treatment would seem merited. By contrast, a rash of newer teams like the lowly Mariners and princely Blue Jays hardly have any history, per se, despite their spectacular soarings or crashes

over the past decade. Yet two newer teams do seemingly cry out to have their stories more fully told. The Montreal Expos and Texas Rangers each potentially provide in full measure all the elements of the exciting team epic. The colorful characters are unquestionably there — Jose "Coco" Laboy and Jeff Burroughs bludgeoning out local legends, Brad Corbett and Bob Short establishing new lows for ownership meddling, Mickey Rivers and Warren Cromartie redefining outfield ineptitude. These teams repeat baseball's favored story of heartbreaking defeat and bungled opportunity. And their present-day plights reflect much about the major-market oriented modern baseball era itself. For fledgling team historians here would seem to be the richest fields to till.

Notes

*Putnam histories cover all pre-expansion-era ballclubs except the Philadelphia Athletics. This gap is both forgiven and explained, however, by the presence of Fred Lieb's 1945 Putnam biography of Connie Mack. In reality the Mack biography is also the missing volume from the team history set. Apparently Putnam editors concluded that Mack was far more marketable (in the mid-'40s) than the ballclub which he owned and managed.

One must certainly concur that any narrative account of the Philadelphia American League club is indeed entirely inseparable in event and substance from the life of the colorful yet dignified figure who guided its fortunes for a full half-century. In short, Connie Mack *was* the Philadelphia Athletics.

Brief Buyer's Guide
to Classic Big League Team Histories

Team history volumes listed below, like those discussed in the above text, are all strictly narrative in format. I have arbitrarily excluded here all those volumes which are largely or exclusively statistical compendiums (such as Bilovsky and Westcott's "The Phillies

Encyclopedia" — just re-done in an impressive updated edition), or mere collections of player profiles (e.g., Tom Meany's "The Boston Red Sox" or Eddie Gold and Art Ahrens' "The Golden Era Cubs" and its two companion volumes), or narrow chronological summaries (Art Berke's "This Date in Chicago White Sox History" and similar volumes devoted to a half-dozen other big league clubs).

While such titles often shed much light on the history of a particular ballclub, they are not "team histories" in the normally accepted sense. Certainly they do not meet the criteria of plotting and character development outlined at the top of this article.

Because I am covering only the major leagues here I have avoided mention of several excellent minor league ballclub histories (Mark Foster's "The Denver Bears: From Sandlots to Sellouts" is my personal favorite) or any of the handful of quality histories devoted to moribund Negro league clubs (Janet Bruce's "The Kansas City Monarchs: Champions of Black Baseball," James Bankes' "The Pittsburgh Crawfords: The Lives & Times of Black Baseball's Most Exciting Team," etc.).

The Classic Putnam Series

Putnam histories yet remain the Cadillacs (better still, the Chalmers Roadsters) of the team history genre. This despite their obvious datedness in both historical coverage and prose style. As rare collectibles, they are increasingly scarce and expensive in the used book shops, although ex-library reading copies are still found for reasonable prices. Volumes on the Cardinals, Tigers, Red Sox, Cubs and White Sox fall into the latter category. The Phillie, Pirate and Senator volumes, on the other hand, are as rare as a Cubs or Red Sox World Series challenge and as pricey as a skybox suite.

Allen, Lee. "The Cincinnati Reds: An Informal History." G.P. Putnam's Sons, 1948.
Brown, Warren. "The Chicago Cubs." G. P. Putnam's Sons, 1946.
Brown, Warren. "The Chicago White Sox." G. P. Putnam's Sons, 1952.

Graham, Frank. "The New York Yankees: An Informal History." G. P. Putnam's Sons, 1943.

Graham, Frank. "The Brooklyn Dodgers: An Informal History." G. P. Putnam's Sons, 1945.

Graham, Frank. "The New York Giants: An Informal History of a Great Baseball Club." G. P. Putnam's Sons, 1952.

Kaese, Harold. "The Boston Braves." G. P. Putnam's Sons, 1948.

Lewis, Franklin. "The Cleveland Indians." G. P. Putnam's Sons, 1949.

Lieb, Frederick G. "The St. Louis Cardinals: The Story of a Great Baseball Club." G. P. Putnam's Sons, 1944 (revised edition, 1950).

Lieb, Frederick G. "Connie Mack: Grand Old Man of Baseball." G. P. Putnam's Sons, 1945. (Philadelphia Athletics)

Lieb, Frederick G. "The Detroit Tigers." G. P. Putnam's Sons, 1946.

Lieb, Frederick G. "The Boston Red Sox." G. P. Putnam's Sons, 1947.

Lieb, Frederick G. "The Pittsburgh Pirates." G. P. Putnam's Sons, 1948.

Lieb, Frederick G. "The Baltimore Orioles: An Informal History of a Great Baseball Club." G. P. Putnam's Sons, 1955.

Lieb, Frederick G. and Stan Baumgartner. "The Philadelphia Phillies." G. P. Putnam's Sons, 1953.

Povich, Shirley. "The Washington Senators." G. P. Putnam's Sons, 1954.

Pictorials and Illustrated Histories

Wheeler and Baskin's "The Cincinnati Game" remains in a class by itself among coffee table pictorials. Honig's half-dozen cloned team histories are written in a lively style and are more noteworthy for their fast-paced historical text than for their exclusively black and white photographs (nearly 75% are close-up head shots). Honig's books do, however, provide numerous photos of journeyman ballplayers absent from most other baseball history volumes and are thus a pure delight for true team specialists.

Anderson, William M. "The Detroit Tigers: A Pictorial Celebration of the Greatest Players and Moments in Tigers' History." South Bend, Indiana: Diamond Communications, 1991.

Aylesworth, Thomas. "Baseball's Great Dynasties: The Cubs." Gallery (W. H. Smith), 1990.

Bready, James H. "The Home Team: The Champion Orioles! Or, The Fat and Lean Years of Baltimore Baseball." Baltimore, 1958 (self-published).

Broeg, Bob. "Redbirds: A Century of Cardinal's Baseball." St. Louis: River City Publishers, 1981.

Cole, Milton. "Baseball's Great Dynasties: The Red Sox." Gallery (W. H. Smith), 1990.

Collett, Ritter. "The Cincinnati Reds: A Pictorial History of Professional Baseball's Oldest Team." Virginia Beach, Virginia: Jordan-Powers, 1976.

Duplacey, Thomas and Joseph Romain. "Baseball's Great Dynasties: The Athletics." Gallery (W. H. Smith), 1991. (Philadelphia, Kansas City and Oakland Athletics)

Durant, John. "The Dodgers: An Illustrated Story of Those Unpredictable Bums." Hastings House, 1948. (Brooklyn Dodgers)

Falls, Joe. "The Detroit Tigers: An Illustrated History." Walker and Company, 1989 (Prentice-Hall, 1990).

Finch, Frank. "The Los Angeles Dodgers: The First Twenty-Five Years." Virginia Beach, Virginia: Jordan-Powers, 1977.

Gallagher, Mark and Neil Gallagher. "Baseball's Great Dynasties: The Yankees." Gallery (W. H. Smith), 1990.

Gutman, Bill. "Baseball's Great Dynasties: The Mets." Gallery (W. H. Smith), 1991.

Kaplan, Jim. "Baseball's Great Dynasties: The Giants." Gallery (W. H. Smith), 1991. (New York and San Francisco Giants)

Honig, Donald. "The Brooklyn Dodgers: An Illustrated Tribute." St. Martin's Press, 1983.

Honig, Donald. "Los Angeles Dodgers: The First Quarter Century." St. Martin's Press, 1983.

Honig, Donald. "The New York Mets: The First Quarter-Century." Crown Publishers, 1986.

Honig, Donald. "The Boston Red Sox: An Illustrated History."

Prentice-Hall, 1990.

Honig, Donald. "The Chicago Cubs: An Illustrated History." Prentice-Hall, 1991.

Honig, Donald. "The St. Louis Cardinals: An Illustrated History." Prentice-Hall, 1991.

Honig, Donald. "The Cincinnati Reds: An Illustrated History." Simon and Schuster, 1992.

Honig, Donald. "The Philadelphia Phillies: An Illustrated History." Simon and Schuster, 1992.

Lang, Jack and Peter Simon. "The New York Mets: Twenty-Five Years of Baseball Magic." Henry Holt, 1986.

Lewis, Allen. "The Philadelphia Phillies: A Pictorial History." Virginia Beach, Virginia: Jordan-Powers, 1981.

Schoor, Gene. "A Pictorial History of the Dodgers: From Brooklyn to Los Angeles." Leisure Press, 1984.

Smizik, Robert. "The Pittsburgh Pirates: An Illustrated History." Walker and Company, 1990.

Wheeler, Lonnie and John Baskin. "The Cincinnati Game." Wilmington, Ohio: Orange Frazer Press, 1988. (Cincinnati Reds)

Whittingham, Richard. "The Los Angeles Dodgers: An Illustrated History." Harper and Row, 1983.

Whittingham, Richard. "The White Sox: A Pictorial History." Chicago: Contemporary Books, 1983.

Forgotten Gems and Selected 'Also Rans'

While most books in the below category provide genuine team chronicles, a handful admittedly emphasize only a single (though usually major) epoch of franchise history. Volumes by Rosenbaum and Stevens, King, Mehl, and Zimmerman are all obvious spin-offs of contemporary franchise relocations, such as the Dodger and Giant arrivals on the west coast or the Athletic relocation in Kansas City. All below works, however, are either tightly enough written or contain enough solid detail on franchise development to merit attention from serious team history buffs.

Bealle, Morris. "The Washington Senators: The Story of an Incurable Fandom." Washington, D.C.: Columbia, 1947.

Beard, Gordon. "Birds on the Wing: The Story of the Baltimore Orioles." Garden City, Doubleday, 1967.

Berry, Henry. "Baseball's Great Teams: The Boston Red Sox." Rutledge (Collier-Macmillan), 1975.

Bilovsky, Frank and Rich Westcott. "The Phillies Encyclopedia." West Point, Leisure Press, 1984.

Borst, Bill. "Still Last in the American League: The St. Louis Browns Revisited." West Bloomfield, Michigan: Altwerger and Mandel, 1992.

Buege, Bob. "The Milwaukee Braves: A Baseball Eulogy." Milwaukee: Douglas American Sports Publications, 1988.

Cohen, Stanley. "Dodgers! The First Hundred Years." Birch Lane Press, 1990. (Brooklyn and Los Angeles Dodgers)

Clark, Tom. "Champagne and Baloney: The Rise and Fall of Finley's A's." Harper and Row, 1976. (Oakland Athletics)

Condon, Dave. "The Go Go Chicago White Sox." Coward-McCann, 1960.

Durso, Joseph. "Amazing: The Miracle of the Mets." Boston: Houghton Mifflin, 1970.

Ellard, Harry. "Base Ball in Cincinnati: A History." Cincinnati, 1907 (self-published). Reprinted by Ohio Book Store, 1987.

Fox, Larry. "Last to First: The Story of the Mets." Harper and Row, 1970.

Golenbock, Peter. "Bums: An Oral History of the Brooklyn Dodgers." G. P. Putnam's Sons, 1984.

Golenbock, Peter. "Fenway: An Unexpurgated History of the Boston Red Sox." G. P. Putnam's Sons, 1992.

Higgins, George V. "The Progress of the Seasons: Forty Years of Baseball in Our Town." Henry Holt, 1989. (Boston Red Sox)

Holmes, Tommy. "Baseball's Great Teams: The Dodgers." Rutledge (Collier-Macmillan), 1975.

Hynd, Noel. "The Giants of the Polo Grounds: The Glorious Times of Baseball's New York Giants." Doubleday, 1988.

King, Joe. "The San Francisco Giants." Englewood-Cliffs, New Jersey: Prentice-Hall, 1958.

Koppett, Leonard. "The New York Mets: The Whole Story." Collier-Macmillan, 1970.

Langford, Jim. "The Game Is Never Over: An Appreciative History of the Chicago Cubs, 1948-1980." South Bend, Indiana: Icarus Press, 1980.

Lindberg, Richard. "Stuck on the Sox." Evanston, Illinois: Sassafras Press, 1978. (Chicago White Sox)

Lindberg, Richard. "Who's on Third? The Chicago White Sox Story." South Bend, Indiana: Icarus Press, 1983.

Lindberg, Richard. "Stealing First in a Two-Team Town: The White Sox From Comiskey to Reinsdorf." Champaign, Illinois: Sagamore, 1994.

Mann, Jack. "The Decline and Fall of the New York Yankees." Simon and Schuster, 1967.

Mehl, Ernest. "The Kansas City Athletics." Henry Holt, 1956.

Mitchell, Jerry. "The Amazing Mets." Grosset and Dunlap, 1970.

Newhan, Ross. "The California Angels: The Complete History." Simon and Schuster, 1982.

Pluto, Terry. "The Curse of Rocky Colavito: A Loving Look at a 30-Year Slump." Simon and Schuster, 1994. (Cleveland Indians)

Rains, Rob. "The St. Louis Cardinals: The 100th Anniversary History." St. Martin's Press, 1992.

Richeal, Kip. "The Pittsburgh Pirates: Still Walking Tall." Champaign, Illinois: Sagamore, 1993.

Rogers, Phil. "The Impossible Takes a Little Longer: The Texas Rangers From Pretenders to Contenders." Dallas, Texas: Taylor, 1990.

Rosenbaum, Art and Bob Stevens. "The Giants of San Francisco." Coward-McCann, 1963.

Shaughnessy, Dan. "The Curse of the Bambino." Dutton (Penguin Books), 1990. (Boston Red Sox)

Turner, Dan. "The Expos Inside Out." Toronto and London: McClelland and Stewart, 1983. (Montreal Expos)

Vanderberg, Bob. "Sox: From Lane and Fain to Zisk and Fisk." Chicago: Chicago Review Press, 1984. (Chicago White Sox)

Vecsey, George. "Joy in Mudville: Being a Complete Account of the Unparalleled History of the New York Mets from Their Most Perturbed Beginnings to Their Rise to Glory and Renown." McCall,

1970.

Westcott, Rich and Frank Bilovsky (see Bilovsky). "The New Phillies Encyclopedia." Revised Edition. Philadelphia: Temple University Press, 1993.

Whitfield, Shelby. "Kiss It Good-Bye." Abelard-Schuman, 1973. (Expansion-era Washington Senators and Texas Rangers, 1961-1972)

Zimmerman, Paul. "The Los Angeles Dodgers." Coward-McCann, 1960.

PETER C. BJARKMAN ("Doctor Baseball") has authored six book-length baseball team histories which include: "The Brooklyn Dodgers" (Chartwell, 1992); "Baseball's Great Dynasties: The Dodgers" (Gallery, 1990); "Baseball's Great Dynasties: The Reds" (Gallery, 1991); and "The Toronto Blue Jays" (Gallery, 1990). He edited the Encyclopedia of Major League Baseball: American League, Team Histories (Carroll & Graf, 1993) and the Encyclopedia of Major League Baseball: National League, Team Histories (Carroll & Graf, 1993). He resides in Lafayette, Indiana, and his recent books are "Baseball With A Latin Beat: A History of the Latin American Game" (McFarland) and juvenile biographies of Ernie Banks, Duke Snider and Warren Spahn (Chelsea House).

Calling the Roll

By John Maxymuk

THOSE OF US WHO HAVE A strong interest in the history of Negro League baseball owe a large debt to the small army of researchers who, over the last 25-30 years, have salvaged the stories, images and statistics of a nearly forgotten era when blacks were shut out of "organized" baseball. Robert Peterson's landmark history volume "Only the Ball Was White" (Prentice-Hall, 1970) introduced most of us to the then unknown world of "separate but equal" black baseball. Many researchers have followed that work with their own studies published in mainstream outlets, small press publishers and Society for American Baseball Research (SABR) publications.

One of those researchers is James Riley, author and self-publisher of "The All-Time All Stars of Black Baseball" and "Dandy, Day and the Devil" under the TK Publishers imprint. "The Biographical Encyclopedia of The Negro Baseball Leagues" is the culmination of over 20 years of personal research by Riley. It is a monumental work.

THE BIOGRAPHICAL ENCYCLOPEDIA OF THE NEGRO BASEBALL LEAGUES
By James A. Riley
Carroll & Graf, 1994, 906 pp. $29.95
through 12/94, $39.95 thereafter

Until now, the only published register of names from Negro League baseball was in an appendix to Peterson's book. That handy catalog listed approximately 900-1,000 players and officials with the positions they played or held, their years of activity and the teams to which they were connected. Riley's work contains over 4,000 names, and not only does it list teams and years of activity, but it indicates what years were spent with which teams as well. Where available, birth and/or death dates and places are included as are height, weight, "bats" and

"throws" data. Finally, there is a biographical narrative of varying length for each entry.

Riley's work is drawn primarily from personal interviews with living players and from combing the archives of newspapers from the time period. In his explanatory notes, Riley claims that "every player who played with a team of major league quality or whose career had historical significance" is included. Thus, Maurice Wiggins is included and his career denoted as a backup shortstop for the Chicago American Giants in 1920; Clarence Everett is included and his career denoted as a shortstop for the Kansas City Monarchs and Detroit Stars in 1927. Neither player has his longer career spent with the Gilkerson Giants mentioned because the Gilkersons were an independent barnstorming team closer to semi-pro quality. On the other hand, a more important player like Bill Evans, a one-time starter on the Homestead Grays and other Negro League teams, has his Gilkerson Giant background fully documented here as part of his career.

There are bound to be inconsistencies between this and other works on the obscured field of dreams that was black baseball. In Peterson's register Wiggins is not listed at all and Everett is listed without a first name and only as a Monarch; this can be taken as a sign of the advancement of current research. More problematic is a case like Eugene White who is listed by Peterson as being on the 1950 Chicago American Giants and is not listed at all by Riley. And the Hancock brothers are a little tricki-

> ## *This work is a giant leap forward as a reference tool.*

er still. Catcher Charlie is listed by both Peterson and Riley as having caught for the St. Louis Giants in 1921; first baseman-outfielder-pitcher Art is listed only by Riley as playing for two Cleveland teams in 1926-27. Phil Dixon and Patrick J. Hannigan, however, in their wonderful book "The Negro Baseball Leagues: A Photographic History" (Amereon, 1992) say the Hancocks never played League ball, but instead stuck to such independents as the Colored House of David.

Essentially, these inconsistencies highlight the difficulty of researching a topic where the contemporary written record is so sketchy. In general, I would take Riley to be the definitive source for questions of this sort. Not only does his book flesh out the existing knowledge base, but he has added so much more. The work is replete with new

names — many partial like "Parks" and "Ping" two players from the deadball era — and offers new directions for further research.

Riley covers a period from pioneer Bud Fowler's alleged beginnings in 1872 to the virtual end of the Negro Leagues in 1950. Though the Negro American League continued on into the 1960s, it no longer met the criterion of major league quality. There are exceptions to the 1950 closing date. Hank Aaron, Ernie Banks and Oscar Charleston (who had a managing stint in 1955) are simply too prominent to exclude on chronological grounds. Others like Buck O'Neil, Dizzy Dismukes, King Tut, Red Longley and Joe Fillmore had careers which continued on unbroken into the declining years of league ball. However, a lesser light like Rufus Ligon who pitched for the Memphis Red Sox from 1944-46, does not have his mid-'50s managing term mentioned. Likewise, Kansas City Monarch founder and longstanding owner J.L. Wilkinson obviously has an entry, as does Tom Baird, his long-time associate who bought J.L. out in 1948. However, there is no entry for Ted Rasberry who in turn bought out Baird in the 1950s. Entries are also included for Toni Stone, Connie Morgan and Peanuts Johnson, three mid-'50s players of

less than stellar quality, but who fit the "historical significance" criterion — they were all women infielders employed by teams in the league to hype the gate.

The greatest strength of this encyclopedia is the richness of the biographical narratives. In these narratives, there is a remarkable level of detail on playing and (sometimes) living styles, especially for the better players. Of Frank Duncan, veteran catcher for the Kansas City Monarchs, we gather that he was a "master of handling pop flies...had a quick release, but threw a 'heavy' ball...was slow on the bases...a line drive hitter..." Of Vic Harris, outfielder and manager of the famed Homestead Grays, we learn "the lefthanded batter was a consistent spray hitter with a short compact swing...a good hit-and-run man...had only moderate power and a bit of a weakness on high fastballs...a good fielder in each phase of the game...not noted as a brilliant strategist...players responded to his fiery leadership." We are informed that star third baseman Jud Wilson was "considered one of the 'Big Four of the big badmen' of black baseball. The others...Chippy Britt, Oscar Charleston, and Vic Harris." For Monarch ace pitcher Hilton Smith, we are given a rundown of his repertoire. "In addition to his superlative curves, he had a high hard fastball that 'took off,' a sinker, a slider, and a change of

pace, all of which he threw both sidearm or overhand, maintaining good control with both styles of delivery."

When available, statistics and batting order slot are worked into the text to give a more objective indication of talent levels. Second baseman George Scales played for the Homestead Grays in 1930-31 and "batted fifth in the order, hitting behind Judy Johnson the first year and Josh Gibson the latter year while recording averages of .303 and .393."

Team histories are featured for league squads and independents of major league quality. Interesting facts are also plentiful. Monarch outfielder Eddie Dwight's "son became the first black American selected for training as an astronaut by NASA, and later gained further recognition as the sculptor of the Hank Aaron statue in Atlanta's Fulton County Stadium." In 1958, expatriate former Baltimore Black Sox outfielder Bill Wright "appeared as one of the surprise guests on television's 'This Is Your Life' show when [Roy Campanella] was the spotlighted celebrity; he was Campy's first roomie. That was Wright's last visit to the United States until 1990 when he attended a reunion of Negro League players."

There are occasional informed editorial comments, "Smokey Joe Williams is the greatest player not yet enshrined in the National Baseball Hall of Fame." "There has never been a more masterful third baseman than Ray Dandridge." And fascinating stories fill the pages. Of owner Alex Pompez Riley writes,

By this time Pompez was an important member of Dutch Schultz's mob and was one of the wealthiest men in Harlem. When Thomas E. Dewey, district attorney of the New York County, began a crackdown on New York racketeers, he selected Pompez as one of his targets, and in 1936, Pompez was indicted by a grand jury for his involvement in policy rackets. Tipped off by an elevator operator while on his way into Dewey's trap, Pompez disappeared, giving rise to rumors that he had been kidnapped or was in hiding to avoid the grand jury's jurisdiction. Actually he escaped to Mexico, where he resumed his flamboyant lifestyle until arrested by Mexican authorities as he was stepping into a bulletproof sedan with Chicago license plates. Mexican officials refused Dewey's request for extradition, but

Pompez decided to return to the United States to turn state's evidence. He is considered to be the only man who informed on another racketeer and lived.

A story regarding Chicago American Giant outfielder Pete Hill reflects the keen competition between top teams.

In 1915, in a hotly contested game against the Indianapolis ABCs, with heavy betting on the outcome [Hill] became engaged in an argument with the umpire, who pulled a gun and hit Hill on the nose. A riot ensued and the game was forfeited to the ABCs.

Other stories are possibly apocryphal. Manager Candy Jim Taylor "had a reputation of being a good judge of young talent, but according to one source, he made a colossal mistake in one instance. In 1930, while managing the Memphis Red Sox, he picked up a youngster named Josh Gibson for a game in Scranton, Pennsylvania, and afterward said that he would never be a catcher."

Riley is a better researcher than stylist, but the reader is sometimes left wondering what happened to certain players after the 1950 cutoff, and the basic ht/wt/bats/throws data is too often unavailable. These problems are understandable and small in relation to the size of his triumphant accomplishment. Clearly photographs would add something to the layout, but also quite a bit to the already ample 906 pages which is probably why they are not included. (Just read this book with Dixon/Hannigan close by.) The thoroughly researched text is the focus, and this work is a giant leap forward as a reference tool.

While it's true that in the last 25 years, there have been many fine books published on black baseball, James Riley's sensational effort in "The Biographical Encyclopedia of the Negro Leagues" joins the pantheon: Peterson, Dixon/Hannigan and John Holway's first oral history volume "Voices From the Great Black Baseball Leagues." Who were those forgotten heroes? Find out here.

JOHN MAXYMUK is a librarian and writer whose first book (not on baseball) is being published this year.

It's A Matter of A(l)ttitude

By Tim Sears

THE TASK OF CHRONICLING the failures and foibles of an expansion team in their first year of existence is intriguing in nature. Capturing the essence and qualities of a team certain to lose, and worse yet, a team without an identity born of history, will challenge the best baseball writer and thinker. It takes a masterful stroke of the pen to make the art of losing both informative and enjoyable.

In general, books that cover winning teams are marketable and books on losing teams are a hard sell. However that does not mean that biographies of struggling teams are always failures. The 1962 Mets have taken a legendary status in baseball folklore largely because of the team bios that captured the camaraderie and hopelessness of the most futile team in modern baseball history. On the flip side, it seems reasonable to assume that the biographies of the '62 Mets were interesting reading because the team was filled with interesting players and a legendary manager, going through their trials of ineptitude in the white-hot media center of New York.

So when an author opts to recount the events of a losing team, he must make sure he achieves two objectives. First, he must choose a team that will have a large fan base. Second, he must find a way to make losing exciting for the average reader. Bob Kravitz, in "Mile High Madness: A Year with the Colorado Rockies" definitely achieves the first objective. The team in the mountains were celebrities long before they ever played a ball game. The fact that the city of Denver and surrounding areas shattered the all-time season attendance record with 4,483,350 fans insures that

---

MILE HIGH MADNESS
By Bob Kravitz
Times Books, 1994, 320 pp., $22

this book will have a niche in the baseball market. For Rocky Mountain baseball zealots and fanatics this book is mandatory reading. The book will easily satisfy the insatiable hunger of Rockie fans.

Only three teams in the past 37 years have crossed the 5.00 ERA mark. (Shall we call it the Sweetland-Willoughby-Line?)

Kravitz chose to write it in a journal format which covers the Rockies from the city's bid for an expansion franchise to the series finale with the Atlanta Braves. This day-by-day approach is both the book's greatest strength and its noisiest weakness. Kravitz covers vast amounts of information on a variety of subjects.

In the Rockies inaugural season they had plenty to be proud of and this book will allow fans to relive those moments. Opening Day at Mile High Stadium was a golden moment in Denver baseball history. Kravitz's description of the event allows the reader to feel the bolts of electrical energy as the record-setting crowd releases years of pent-up baseball energy with Eric Young's home run in the first ever at-bat in home history. Fans will also revel in the remarkable turnaround of Andres Galarraga and his quest for .400, which eventually fell short, but still resulted in the National League batting title, the first ever won by an expansion player.

However a synopsis of a year with any expansion team is hardly a celebration of greatness and triumphant moments. Such a book would not accurately depict the '93 Rockies. The faithful will be both enchanted and dismayed when the weaknesses are painfully uncovered. The shortcomings on the playing field were obvious. The team was exciting to watch thanks to the hitter-friendly "confines" of the ballpark, but the pitching suffered the other edge of the sword, getting hit hard and often.

In fact, the Rockie team ERA of 5.41 deserves some historical credit. Forty-two seasons have come and gone since a team's staff got belted around so handily. Only three teams in the past 37 years have crossed the team 5.00 ERA mark. (Shall we call it the Willoughby-Sweetland Line?) One was the '62 Mets, and the others happened in 1987, the Year of the Cork.

The Rockies' weaknesses on the field were widely publicized during

the regular season, but what Kravitz uncovers in his book are inner blemishes that revealed a team in discontent, not a bunch of happy-go-lucky schmoes enjoying their season in the sun. The dings in the Rockie armor were both plentiful and ugly. The attitudes and actions of the 1993 Rockies reflect and mirror the myriad of problems that face baseball.

Kravitz quickly lays to rest the romantic cliche that an expansion ballclub represents baseball in its purest form. The utopia-expansion theory states that expansion players are free from the corruption that infects baseball. It states that desire, not money, motivates the players, which allows them to play purely for the love of the game. It isn't true, or at least it wasn't in Denver last year.

Outfielder Darryl Boston is labeled a classic underachiever willing to do just enough to retain a spot on a major league roster. Rockie star third baseman Charlie Hayes is portrayed as a lackadaisical player who has not tapped his full potential, and probably never will. Even pitching phenom David Nied is briefly depicted as a complainer and backbiter (although not in the Pedro Borbon sense) The book also hones in on a feud between third base coach Jerry Royster and manager Don Baylor. Kravitz explains how the Rockies must look for not just talent, but also the right mix of people, and how it isn't automatic, or easy.

Unlike the team it covers, this book is strongest at the beginning. The "Rockie phenomenon" is vividly depicted. The coverage of

> ## When the Rockies had a chance to play the role of spoiler in a rugged pennant race, they rolled over and played dead.

the city's bid for an expansion franchise unveils the sense of pride the locals hold. The profiles of manager Baylor, GM Bob Gebhard and consultant Bob Howsam are warm and colorful. Every fan will enjoy reading about how the Rockies were created, from just a name and a logo to a full roster. The construction of an expansion franchise is fascinating, and Kravitz is entertaining throughout. The book serves as a navigating instrument as the reader follows the club from the promotional team caravans through the Rocky Mountain region to the

expansion draft, to spring training, and the final roster cuts.

Once the season is underway and the team fully in place the book slips into the abyss of a losing season. Kravitz does an admirable job of trying to perk up the Rockies miserable first half by comparing the team to the New York Mets, spending time in summaries of the battles between their expansion sisters the Florida Marlins and the newly-miserable Mets for last place. Eventually these lengthy summaries wear thin and become trite as the Rockies put it together in the second half of the season.

They completed the 1993 season with the best National League record for an expansion club, losing only 95 games. But while the Rockies picked up speed in the second half, this book does not. When the Rockies had a chance to play the role of spoiler in a rugged pennant race, they rolled over and played dead. The book covers the Brave series but only in a brief and uninspiring way.

"Mile High Fever" is full of what Rockie fans want. But for the rest of us, once the team takes the field, all we have is another book about a bad team in the 1990s.

TIM SEARS is a freelance writer and editor of "The Royal Proclamation — A Magazine Dedicated to KC Royal fans."

He Settles into a Groove

By Len Levin

THERE'S LITTLE IN BOB Carroll's amusing little tome that you don't already know if you're knowledgeable enough about baseball to be reading this journal. After all, how many more times do you need to be told that Abner Doubleday didn't really invent baseball, that Babe Herman didn't really triple into a triple play, that Babe Ruth didn't really call his shot in the 1932 World Series, or that more than a few citizens of the Hall of Fame should be deported, or at least demoted from great to merely good?

The title overreaches; the book is far from a "Baseball Confidential." And its early chapters are written in an annoyingly smarmy tone. But Carroll is a tease. He's like a pitcher who can't find the plate at the outset, then settles into a groove. By the time he reaches the middle chapters, he's offering some genuine insights, and he may change your longstanding opinions on at least a couple of aspects of the game.

You wouldn't expect, for instance, to see the 1927 Yankees listed among the five most overrated major league teams, but Carroll makes a pretty good case for inclusion. Call them "one of the greatest teams of all time," he concedes, "but The Greatest? I don't think so." Despite Ruth's 60 dingers, Gehrig's 175 RBIs, Combs's .356 batting, the Yankees' 975 runs were only the 11th best in major league history; the pitching staff would have been mediocre with only an average offense behind it; the fielding was ordinary, and the bench was weak.

BASEBALL BETWEEN THE LIES:
THE HYPE, HOKUM AND HUMBUG OF AMERICA'S FAVORITE PASTIME
By Bob Carroll
Perigee Books, 1994, 237 pp., paper, $12

The 1929-31 A's, Carroll says, were better all around. The '36 Yankees were better than the '27 team.

In fact, forget about calling any pre-World War II team the greatest. "How can a team be the greatest

---

> ## [By] Carroll's reasoning the Archduke, who most assuredly never saw a curveball in his life, is responsible for baseball's lively-ball era.

---

ever," Carroll sensibly argues, "when it never had to face a significant number of the best players in America?" Of course he means Satchel Paige, Buck Leonard, et al. "In my book... there can't be a pre-Jackie Robinson 'best ever.' Anything monochrome is overrated." Right on.

Carroll's best chapters, in my view, are the ones in which he wields his debunking sword at the All-Star Game, explains Babe Ruth's rise to greatness in a way it's never been done before, and

explores the unending appeal of baseball trivia.

When the All-Star Game was begun in the pre-television early '30s, Carroll says, it was "a big deal that could really heat up your blood... a moment to be anticipated, savored and remembered." Sixty years later, it's become "baseball's biggest bore." A harsh indictment, but Carroll backs up his charge.

The All-Star game began to go off the tracks in 1957, when Cincinnati fans stuffed the ballot boxes and engineered the election of seven Reds — all but their first baseman — to the starting lineup, and Commissioner Ford Frick compounded the disaster by summarily de-electing Wally Post and Gus Bell, then returning the selection of the starting lineups from the fans to the players and managers — "in effect removing the only good reason to hold an All-Star game in the first place." (Bowie Kuhn returned the franchise to the fans in 1970. Ballot-stuffing hasn't entirely disappeared, but it's not as blatant as in the Cincinnati summer of 1957.)

Of course, neither system of selection is perfect; seven players didn't make their all-star squads the year they were their league's MVP. But that's far from the worst of the All-Star Game's problems.

The worst, pure and simple, is greed, compounded by the lure of TV. While greed can be an almost noble motivating force in business,

it's poison to a sport as noble in form as baseball, and it's almost completely enveloped the All-Star Game. This process began in 1960-62 when there were two games each season, about a month apart. (Carroll doesn't say, but my recollection is that the second game was scheduled with the connivance of the players, who wanted the extra money for their pension fund.)

The two-game setup mercifully — for the fans — perished quickly, but the owners, seldom noted for foresight and prodded by the TV interests, soon began to regard the Game as just another cash cow. Like the World Series, it's now played in prime time. While a game that should be baseball's premier midseason showcase is on the air, a whole generation of future fans is asleep.

Perhaps it's just as well, Carroll writes, because the All-Star Game has become "one of the most boring games of the summer."

"A close, low-hit game during the season can be exciting because there's something at stake — even if it's only the pitcher's ERA. But, with the All-Star Game, there's no suspense because the outcome doesn't matter. All you can do is hope one of the endless parade of pitchers won't have it tonight so you can finally see some hitting..." Not quite true the last two Games

— 13-6 in 1992 and 9-3 in 1993 — but the Game has had an amazing run of low-scoring results. Arch Ward, if you could see your baby now!

As for Babe Ruth, he's the greatest hitter and run-producer no matter what statistical measurement you use, says Carroll, and the ill-fated Archduke Ferdinand, whose assassination touched off World War I, gets most of the credit. (In fact, if you follow Carroll's reasoning the Archduke, who most assuredly never saw a curveball in his life, is responsible for baseball's lively-ball era — in fact for all the paths along which the sport has developed since the War to End All Wars.)

Pitcher Ruth's all-out swing, a rarity for those dead-ball, contact-hitting days, had remained unchanged since he arrived in the Show full time in 1915. In 1918, with many major leaguers off to the World War or doing defense work, the Red Sox were short of outfielders, and the Babe soon found himself spending as much time in the outfield as on the mound. Showman-team owner Harry Frazee's need for a bankroll and the establishment's recognition that home runs, especially Ruth's, brought in the customers made "Ruthian" an adjective and gave us the game we have today.

The chapter on trivia is a short but delightful section in which, for the first time ever (I think), the rules of baseball trivia are formalized. They're as succinct, but not quite as epic, as the Ten Commandments. They number only four: 1) Studying is not allowed; 2) Questions must encompass the era during which the answerer has followed baseball; 3) Answers should be names, not numbers; and 4) Answers should be unique, surprising or amusing. Any other rules are simply corollaries of the foregoing four.

Carroll picks some nits along the way. He believes many 19th-century records, particularly for pitching victories, are relatively meaningless when compared with today's records. He debunks the debunkers of Tinker, Evers and Chance. His contrarian views flavor much of his text.

Even so, the tone of the book is largely upbeat. And even as he hurls his cynic's darts at baseball, Carroll can't conceal his love of the game. This is a lot of fun.

LEN LEVIN is an editor at the Providence (R.I.) Journal, the custodian of SABR's Research Library, and an ardent believer that in the perfect world to come, Babe Ruth and Sparky Lyle will still be with the Red Sox.

What Do Women Think?

by Glenn Stout

I N A YEAR IN WHICH A WOMAN proves she can pitch at the collegiate level, and a women's professional baseball team is in the works, it seems completely appropriate for a book like "Diamonds Are A Girl's Best Friend" to be published. What's surprising is that no one did so before. All in all, while it's a fine and worthy effort, this isn't quite the book it should have been.

The book contains seventy-five poems, short stories, essays and excerpts from novels, all written by women and, to varying degrees, containing references to baseball. Nauen does well in exposing the general reader to many writers he or she may previously have been unfamiliar with. Likewise, she is to be commended for including such a substantial selection of poetry, which is too often either over-

**DIAMONDS ARE A
GIRL'S BEST FRIEND:**
Women Writers on Baseball
Edited by Elinor Nauen
Faber and Faber, 1994, 295 pp., $22.95

looked or diminished in other baseball anthologies.

But the creation of an anthology is more than simply making certain one covers all the bases of form and, like a small town newspaper, gets all the names in. In the really good anthology, every piece should aspire toward a similar standard of excellence. Nothing should be included simply because it meets a criterion. Likewise, the successful anthology should avoid, as much as possible, the predictable and expected. As an anthologist myself, I know this goal isn't easy or (even) always possible; we're usually judged by the worst piece in the book. But it should always be the goal.

Another important consideration is freshness. Enjoyable as they are, for instance, Charles Einstein's Fireside series and John Thorn's Armchair series both suffer from

the same failure; too much dependence upon work that is already familiar. I've never had the sense with either series, much beyond the first edition, that either editor was much concerned with reading the

The one glaring omission is writing by female sports journalists.

obscure to find something really spectacular. In contrast, the selections in Richard Grossinger and Kevin Kerrane's numerous anthologies have always been anything but predictable. I find each of them almost revelatory for precisely this reason.

Nauen's failure in these two areas leads directly to the problem with this collection. For every selection or two that is of quality and sometimes even wondrous (see Molly O'Neill's story on her major league outfielder brother Paul, or Barbara Grizzuti Harrison on Red Barber), there is a piece that is not only a cut below the others, but sometimes embarrassing.

In her introduction Nauen states that "I worried that I'd have to use every scrap I could lay my hands on; I was delighted and surprised at how much material there turned out to be. While I tried to be inclusive and various, if I liked a piece it went in, if I didn't it didn't." Reading the anthology, too many selections seem thrown in simply because of one or two, sometimes awkward, or worse yet, inaccurate, baseball references. They come across as simply writing by a woman that mentions baseball, precisely the scraps Nauen seeks to avoid, and not an example of a woman writing on baseball. Why for instance, include one uninspiring paragraph from Letty Cottin Pogrebin's 1991 memoir "Deborah, Golda and Me: Being Female and Jewish in America," wherein she thanks her cousin Danny for teaching her about baseball? I mean, gee Dan, that was real nice of you, but this paragraph is hardly a stellar example of women writing on baseball. For the life of me, I can't figure out why Nauen liked this paragraph or about a dozen or so other selections so much. If she really was surprised by the amount of material out there, why were pieces like this included?

Likewise, the inclusion of some too familiar work, usually by poets, further undercuts the strength of this anthology. Included herein the reader will find the standard baseball poems by Marianne Moore,

May Swenson and others that have been included in many other collections. Such pieces have reached familiarity simply because they were selected through puerile tokenism for anthologies put together by men. They are neither great examples of baseball writing or representative of the poets' work. Including them in this book seems to me to demean what the anthology hopes to accomplish.

While there are some other, fine examples of poetry included, there are also a number that sound as if they were written by what poet Jack Spicer called "the English Department." "The baseball part" is often contrived, awkward, and extraneous. I just don't get the sense that Nauen looked too hard to find them, but chose what was readily available to her. Baseball poems by women have been regularly popping up in small press magazines for the last twenty years. I myself have found dozens. Most that are in this book appeared in the university or small press only in the last five or six years or are culled from other baseball anthologies and literary baseball publications.

The one glaring omission is writing by female sports journalists. Only a handful are included, and I think Nauen, who focuses primarily on the literary, missed much fine work from this area. Where are Joan Ryan, Jennifer Briggs, and the many other female sports journalists of note? Nauen also inexplicably excludes memoirs written by female baseball figures with the help of a male sportswriter. Were these women all too weak to have influenced the product of their collaboration? That's a dangerous supposition. Given the way publishing is, I suspect that the majority of the selections in the book saw the hand of a male editor, and I'm pretty certain one selection in the book, by Mabel Hite from Baseball Magazine, was ghost-written by a man, so I don't quite get the exclusion.

This book has been widely reviewed, and each review I've seen has been absolutely, and I think, incorrectly, fawning, as if the subject matter alone made any review but a rave too risky. I find such coddling by reviewers patronizing and a bit offensive. The "girls," I think, deserve a more considered reading.

I wish this anthology had been cut by perhaps one-third. It would have been a better book, and I'd have liked it more. For after reading this collection, the question has yet to be answered: well, what about women writing on baseball? Do women have a different perspective? Do they write about baseball differently than men? By undercutting the collection with too many sub-par selections, Nauen leads the door open to come to a conclusion that, too often, too many women

apparently don't write very well about baseball, and when they do, they write about it in distressingly similar fashion about their: a) father, b) lover, c) brother, or d) grandparent. I don't think this conclusion is either correct, or the one Nauen was hoping for.

There is another anthology out there still to be put together, or perhaps another edition of this one that is more selective and might include other fine work originally missed. That book, perhaps, will better demonstrate that just as women are capable of playing baseball, they are also capable of writing well about it. The diamond simply isn't a girls' best friend, a bauble draped over the typing finger. To many women, as most of the selections in this book demonstrate, it is much more. Those writers deserve a book more cognizant of that reality.

In addition to being a regular contributor to this publication, GLENN STOUT is Series Editor for Houghton Mifflin's annual "The Best American Sports Writing."

Marvin Said So

By Paul Adomites

I T IS TRUE THAT THE RICH ARE different from you and me. The other night my wife and I were out for supper when we saw a business acquaintance of some means and his spouse. In friendly style we sent them a cock-tail. They recipro-cated by buying our dinner.

But I must say another thought occurred to me while I read John Helyar's "Lords of the Realm," the hot new book that describes in gory detail the behind the scenes awfulness that has always been part of the Game's history. I have been in the business world for more than 25 years, and I've dealt with all kinds of people, not a few of them highly successful, highly motivated, hard charging million-aires. Some made their dough by being in the right place at the right time, others by ingenuity and great ideas, others just by sheer force of

LORDS OF THE REALM:
The Real History of Baselll
By John Helyar
Villard, 1994, 576 pp., $20

will. But in all those years through all those meetings and dealings, I have never met anywhere as many venal, crude, smug, egotistical, proud-to-be-bastards as the average bartender could easily swat with a swizzle stick at any meeting of base-ball owners. Sure, I've run across a few. But their phoniness and noise was usually easy to ignore when it came down to doing the job. If I come across one nowadays, I just don't deal with him or her. Life is too short.

My experience, in fact, has indi-cated that most business people (given the fears and frailties we all face) try hard to do what's right and to do a good job, and while not all can be credited with long-term thinking excellence, they usually understand what is on their plate with unerring precision.

Then why does baseball, and

why has it always, attracted the sorts of folk we read about in "Lords of the Realm"? These individuals are not just misguided; they are absolutely loony, fueled by an exaggerated sense of their own relevance. It's not that they fail to see the value of coordinated thinking, planning and effort to achieve some reasonable goals; they actually despise the whole notion.

You know the characters; we've all read too much about them already. Marvin Miller, whose ego found an equal match with the owners, but whose intelligence never did. Do you ever wonder how Marvin can sleep at night knowing he did hands-on duty in destroying both the U.S. steel industry and major league baseball? As one character in the book said of him, "Marvin couldn't make a deal. Everything was just a truce on a battlefield." The closest the owners ever got to a bargaining strategy was some variation of "Let's get the #@$#&*%ing players."

Anyone who has been able to read since 1973 already knows more than he wants about Charlie Finley or Bowie Kuhn. Helyar does us the service of reminding us of other antiheroes in this particular morality play whose names might not yet have made our skins crawl or the vomitus rise in our gorges — Jerry Kapstein, Ted Turner, Ray Grebey,

Tom Reich. And of course the Commissioners — what a laughable lot they have been. Even the one with the poet's soul couldn't resist the chance to ride as a white knight into battle with the representative of the dark side who had 4,256 hits.

Helyar traces the "real history" of the Game all the way back to when the first players took pay for having all this fun. We know all this. The Tales of Landis, the Agonies of O'Malley, the Songfests of Happy Chandler have been told many times before. What's remarkable is that the same is true of much of the rest of it. Unlike his previous book (co-authored with Bryan Burrough), "Barbarians At The Gate," which was revelatory in describing the meanness and ugliness of the moguls of the entertainment business, the stories of the inner workings of the baseball power elite have been spilled on the pages of magazines, newspapers and books for years now. (They can't keep their mouths shut.) We know all too well how Miller connived to make these talented athletes multimillionaires while cynically draping himself in a flag of "personal freedom." (Why does an association of millionaires need a pension fund anyway?)

We know how Bowie Kuhn was torn by the fact that he really wanted to do something good for baseball yet had too many powerful bosses to kowtow to. We've heard

how the owners tried over and over again to eliminate the players union, never once getting the message so perfectly delineated by Rudy May, "Don't the owners know there is going to be a whole generation of ballplayers' sons with the middle name of Marvin?" We all know too well that what started out as fiscal responsibility initiated by Commissioner Ueberroth turned into collusion because the owners kept congratulating themselves in public and cautioning players that the gravy train had run out of grease. In fact, Ueberroth's taking charge as a true CEO is one of the few moments in this book that make a reader feel things could have been different. So unless you're a fan of collecting obscene and racist quotes spoken by team owners, there's not much new here, with the possible exception of the most recent struggles within management to decide on revenue sharing.

Who's to blame? Nobody, the conventional wisdom has it. All the participants were acting only "in their own best interests." But that's exactly why they're all to blame. Let's speak facts: the players' insistence on "not taking a step back" is and was absurd. Take enough little steps and you'll go a long way. Isn't it possible, or even wise, to stop at some point, take a look around and evaluate whether this is really where you (and everyone else) should be? Quantitative changes become qualitative changes: stand at the bottom of a hill and let me roll a one-ounce stone at you. You won't even feel it. But if I increase the weight of the stone by an ounce each time, before long it will hurt. And before long it will kill you. "Never give a inch" is not the motto of reasonable people. Life is about giving inches and getting inches. Watch a runner on first in his cat-and-mouse game with the pitcher. The fact is, while the Marvinites were refusing to "step back," they were doing what the owners had always done: ignoring the bigger picture.

You can't fault the owners for ignoring the bigger picture. They have no picture at all. What is the unique mix of frustrated athletic youth and scads of money that creates such amazing behavior? In their chosen fields, many of these men were (are) savvy businessmen, but when it comes to owning a team, their wits were left elsewhere. Helyar points out a truly frightening fact: "By 1981, more than one third of the clubs had owners with less than five years in baseball. They had very different means and markets. But they had common traits: ego, involvement, and ignorance."

It makes us, the fans, the people whose love of the game is deep and profound, angry. And if you are try-

ing to wipe anger from your life in favor of forgiveness and understanding, this book is no place to start.

As a book of history, "Lords of the Realm" belongs on the shelf next to "Judge Landis and 25 Years of Baseball." But it's much too close for me to enjoy just now. Maybe 25 years from now, this era will be laughed upon as the culmination of the underside of the American ideal: the absurd combination of greed and arrogance. Of course that's assuming that there will still be baseball 25 years from now, or at any rate, people who still care about it. I hope that's not too big an assumption.

AN AFTERTHOUGHT: However, I *am* trying to replace anger with forgiveness and understanding, which leads me to consider another approach to all this. If baseball is America, and America is baseball (and they are), then the sport has to underscore our weaknesses as well as our strengths. It has to. And what is a better description of the essential conflict of the American character than this: the battle between 1) the belief that we all have the chance (and even the right) to be rich individualists who don't give a snot for anybody but our own egos and 2) the noble sense of community, generosity, teamwork and the pride of cooperation that really makes things happen? Let's call this ongoing conflict "Cowboys and Indians." Taken in that light, the "Lords" of this book are just characters doing an exceptional job of acting out the roles they are destined to play. In the context of the true big picture, they are just doing their job.

The real bottom line is that until we as a people can sort out the difference between accumulated fiscal assets and real riches, baseball is doomed to keep echoing our incompetence.

PAUL ADOMITES edits this publication and others.